Oxford International English

6

Izabella Hearn
Myra Murby
Moira Brown

OXFORD
UNIVERSITY PRESS

OXFORD
UNIVERSITY PRESS

Great Clarendon Street, Oxford OX2 6DP

Oxford University Press is a department of the University of Oxford.
It furthers the University's objective of excellence in research, scholarship,
and education by publishing worldwide in

Oxford New York

Auckland Cape Town Dar es Salaam Hong Kong Karachi
Kuala Lumpur Madrid Melbourne Mexico City Nairobi
New Delhi Shanghai Taipei Toronto

With offices in

Argentina Austria Brazil Chile Czech Republic France Greece
Guatemala Hungary Italy Japan Poland Portugal Singapore
South Korea Switzerland Thailand Turkey Ukraine Vietnam

© Oxford University Press 2013

British Library Cataloguing in Publication Data

Data available

ISBN- 978-019-838884-5

20 19 18 17 16 15 14 13 12

Printed in India by Manipal Technologies Limited

Paper used in the production of this book is a natural, recyclable product made from wood
grown in sustainable forests. The manufacturing process conforms to the environmental
regulations of the country of origin.

Acknowledgements

The publisher and authors would like to thank the following for permission to use photographs
and copyright material:

p8b: Kobal/BBC/Pathe Films; p8t: Getty Images; p11: Suzanne Long/Alamy; p14: Getty Images/
Tobias Bernhard; p15: Stockbyte/Getty Images; p16: Wild Shutter/Alamy; p22tl: Getty Images/
Hindustan Times; p22:bl: Getty Images; p22br: Getty Images; p22tr: Getty Images/AFP; p23:
Eduard Stelmakh/Shutterstock; p25: imagebroker/Alamy; p28: Getty Images/Barcroft Media;
p29r: Getty Images/Barcroft Media; p29l: Getty Images; p32: Mauro Ujetto/Demotix/Corbis;
p33: Getty Images; p36a: Alamy/Ladi Kifn; p36b: Shi Yali/Shutterstock; p36c: Albrecht Durer/
Bridgeman; p36d: Bridgeman; p37t: Alamy/Zena Elea; p37b: © Franck Goddio; p38: Paul B.
Moore/Shutterstock; p39t&m: Dr A Nombro/Courtesy of admiraltyshipmodels.co.uk; p39b:
Alamy/David Coleman; p42: © Franck Goddio; p43: © Franck Goddio; p44: Maks Narodenko/
Shutterstock; p47: Linda Bucklin/Shutterstock; p48: Corbis; p49: © Hiroya Minakuchi/Minden
Pictures/Corbis; p52tl: Shutterstock/Pius Lee; p52tr: tramways5/Shutterstock; p52b: Alamy/
Corbis Bridge; p53: OUP/Photodisc; p58: ©E.M.Clements; p62t: Michael Ventura/Alamy; p62b:
BennettPhoto/Alamy; p64: Binkski/Shutterstock; p63: Bridgeman Art Library/The Stapleton
Collection; p66r: Kobal/Weinstein & Co; p66l: Kobal/Dimension Films; p67: Kobal/MGM/
Everett; p69: Walker books; p70: Walker book; p72t: ©Tom Gregory; p72b: DK Images; p73t:
Images Etc Ltd/Alamy; p73b: Phillippe Psaila/Science Photo Libraryp74: Miramax/Ricco Torres/
Kobal Collection; p76: © E.M.Clements; p78: Walker Books; p80l: Rex Features/Michael Friedel;
p80r: NASA; p80b & p81: Shutterstock/Todd Shoemake; p81r: Joseph Wright of Derby/Getty
Images; p81b: Marcos81/Shutterstock; p83: Joseph Wright of Derby/Bridgeman/Getty; p86l:
Getty Images/Kevin Schafer; p86r: Getty Images/Juergen Ritterbach; p87: Fotolia; p88: Alamy/
Waterframe; p93: pattyphotoart/Shutterstock; p96tl: © Facundo Arrizabalaga/epa/Corbis;
p96tr: Hulton-Deutsch Collection/Corbis; p96bl: © Tomas Bravo/Reuters/Corbis; p96br: An
advertising print of a circus owned by Hayatake Torakichi, travelling from Osaka to Ryogoku
in Edo, 1845 (colour woodblock print), Kunisada, Utagawa (1786-1864) / School of Oriental &
African Studies Library, Uni. of London / The Bridgeman Art Library; p97: © Walter Lockwood/
Corbis; p102b: Toshifumi Kitamura/Getty; p102t: John Slater/Corbis; p103: © See Li/Demotix/
Corbis; p109: Imeh Akpanudosen/Getty Images; p110tl & br: Shutterstock/R Gino Santa Maria;
p110tr: Getty Images/Richard I'Anson; p110bl: Tetra Images/Alamy; p111: Alamy/Photo Network;
p113: Natalia Hubbert/Shutterstock; p115: AlexanderZam/Shutterstock.com; p116: Andrew
Woodley/Alamy; p118: © Luong Thai Linh/epa/Corbis; p120: Shutterstock/Attem; p121: Ye
Liew/Shutterstock; p122: dollarstorecrafts.com; p124l: istanbulint.com; p124t: Getty Images/
Dream Pictures; p124r: Rtimages/Shutterstock; p124b: © Dan Pangbourne/Image Source/Corbis;
p124r: vovan/Shutterstock; p124r: Alexey Pushkin/Shutterstock; p125: Chris Jobs/Alamy; p130:
Ragnarock/Mitrofanova/Serg64/Ashwin/Markovka/Shutterstock & Art Directors & TRIP/Alamy;
p131: © Sony; p136: Rex Features/Picture Group; p138t&b: Getty Images ; p138l: Fernando
Cortes/Shutterstock; p138r: Morey Milbradt/Alamy; p138t: Blue Jean Images/Alamy; p139t:
Claudia Wiens/Alamy; p139b: Roussel Bernard/Alamy; p144tl: Sanjay Deva/Shutterstock; p144tr:
alersandr hunta/Shutterstock; p144b: Tom Wang/Shutterstock; p148: © Martin Puddy/Corbis;
p151: TongRo Images/Alamy.

Background images: mack2happy/Shutterstock; R-studio/Shutterstock; H2O/Shutterstock;
David M. Schrader/Shutterstock; donatas1205/Shuttertock; Africa Studio/Shutterstock; Qiwen/
Shutterstock; Markovka/Shutterstock; dghagi/Shutterstock.

Cover illustration: Patricia Castelao

Illustrations are by: Stefano Azzalin; Giorgio Bacchin; Stefan Chabluk; Russ Daff; Leicia
Gotlibowsk; Melanie Matthews; Gustavo Mazali; Dusan Pavlic; Scott Plumbe; Giulia Rivolta;
Meilo So; Mike Spoor; Katri Valkamo; Claudia Venturini; Jan Wijngaard.

The author and publisher are grateful for permission to reprint the following copyright
material:

Isaac Asimov: extract from 'The Fun They Had' in *Earth is Room Enough* (Granada, 1981),
copyright © Isaac Asimov 1981, reprinted by permission of the Estate of Isaac Asimov c/o The
Trident Media Group , LLC.

Rhidian Brook: extracts from an unpublished screenplay, *Africa United*, copyright © Rhidian
Brook 2012, used by permission of The Agency (London) Ltd on behalf of the author.

Dave Calder: 'Flood', copyright Dave Calder 1989, from *Dolphins Leap Lampposts, poems by Dave
Calder, Eric Finney and Ian Souter* (Macmillan, 2002), reprinted by permission of the author.

Paul Cookson: 'Let No One Steal Your Dreams' from *The Very Best of Paul Cookson* (Macmillan,
2001), copyright © Paul Cookson 2001, reprinted by permission of the author.

Terry Deary: extract from *The Plot on the Pyramid* (A & C Black, 2004), copyright © Terry Deary
2004, reprinted by permission of the publishers, A & C Black, an imprint of Bloomsbury
Publishing Plc.

John Foster: 'The Price of Fame', copyright © John Foster 2007, from *The Poetry Chest* (OUP,
2007), reprinted by permission of the author.

Clive Gifford: extracts from *Spies and Spying* (OUP, 2010), reprinted by permission of Oxford
University Press.

Anthony Horowitz: extracts from *Stormbreaker: The Graphic Novel* (Walker Books, 2006) based
on the screen play by Anthony Horowitz adapted by Antony Johnston, illustrated by Kanako
and Yuzuru, text and illustrations copyright © 2006 Walker Books Ltd; screenplay © 2006
Samuelsons/IoM Film; Film © 2006 Film and Entertainment VIP Medienfonds 4 GmbH & Co.
KG; Style Guide © 2006 ARR Ltd; Trademarks 2006 Samuelson Productions Ltd, Stormbreaker™
Alex Rider™, Boy with torch logo™, AR logo™; reproduced by permission of Walker Books Ltd,
London, SE11 5HJ, www.walker.co.uk.

Bobbi Katz: 'Heraklion: An Underwater City in the Bay of Abukir off the North Coast of Egypt'
from *Trailblazers: Poems of Exploration* by Bobbi Katz (Greenwillow Books, 2007), copyright ©
Bobbi Katz 2007, reprinted by permission of the author.

Anabel Kindersley: extracts from *Celebration! Celebration! (Children Just Like Me)* (DK, 1997),
copyright © Dorling Kindersley Ltd, 1997, reprinted by permission of Dorling Kindersley Ltd,
London.

John Kitching: 'Historian', copyright © John Kitching 2002, first published in Brian Moses
(ed): *The Works 2: Poems on Every Subject and For Every Occasion* (Macmillan Children's Books, 2002),
reprinted by permission of the author.

Elizabeth Laird: 'Pulling Together' from *Why Dogs Have Black Noses (Oxford Reading Tree, Myths
and Legends*, OUP, 2010), copyright © Elizabeth Laird 2010, reprinted by permission of Oxford
University Press.

Gill Lewis: extract from *White Dolphin* (OUP, 2010), copyright © Gill Lewis 2010, reprinted by
permission of Oxford University Press.

Brian Moses: 'Salute', copyright © Brian Moses 2012, from *Olympic Poems* (by Brian Moses and
Roger Stevens (Macmillan, 2012), used by permission of the author.

National Geographic: Instructions for making a kite from http://kids.nationalgeographic.
com, by permission of National Geographic Stock.

Kenn Nesbitt: 'My Dad's a Secret Agent', copyright © 2001 by Kenn Nesbitt from *The Aliens
Have Landed at Our School* (Meadowbrook, 2001, 2006) and 'When Sarah Surfs the Internet',
copyright © 2007 by Kenn Nesbitt from *Revenge of the Lunch Ladies: the Hilarious Book of School
Poetry* (Meadowbrook, 2007), both reprinted by permission of Meadowbrook Press.

Scott O'Dell: 'The Iditarod Great Sled Race' from *Black Star, Bright Dawn* (Houghton Mifflin
Harcourt, 2008), copyright © Scott O'Dell 1988, by permission of McIntosh and Otis, Inc for the
author.

James Putnam and Scott Steedman: extract from *Egyptian News* (Walker Books, 2009), text
copyright © Scott Steedman 1997, reprinted by permission of Walker Books Ltd, London, SE11
5HJ, www.walker.co.uk.

Noel Streatfeild: extracts from *Circus Shoes* (Jane Nissen Books, 2006), copyright © Noel
Streatfeild 1938, reprinted by permission of A M Heath & Co Ltd for the Estate of Noel
Streatfeild.

Eleanor Watts: 'Who is this?', two kennings, copyright © Eleanor Watts 2012, first published
here by permission of the author.

Kay Woodward: extract from *Skate School: Stars on Ice* (Usborne Books, 2010), copyright ©
Chorion Rights Ltd 2010, reprinted by permission of Usborne Publishing, 83-85 Saffron Hill,
London, EC1N 8RT, UK. www.usborne.com.

WWF-New Zealand: extract from a bulletin about Hector's and Maui's dolphins from www.
wwf.org.nz with figures as at 13 March 2012, reprinted by permission of WWF-New Zealand.

Laurence Yep: extract from *The Star Maker* (HarperCollins, 2010), reprinted by permission of
HarperCollins Publishers, USA.

Although we have made every effort to trace and contact all copyright holders before
publication this has not been possible in all cases. If notified, the publisher will rectify any
errors or omissions at the earliest opportunity.

Contents

A world of stories, poems and facts

ALASKA

NORTH AMERICA

U.S.A

ATLANTIC OCEAN

PACIFIC OCEAN

GALÁPAGOS ISLANDS

SOUTH AMERICA

U KI

AFR

ARCTIC OCEAN

EUROPE

KAZAKHSTAN

ASIA

CHINA

JAPAN

EGYPT

VIETNAM

KENYA

INDIAN
OCEAN

OUTH AFRICA

AUSTRALIA

OCEANIA

NEW ZEALAND

ERN OCEAN

Unit contents

Language, grammar, spelling, vocabulary, phonics	Writing	Speaking and listening
• Sentence length and structure • Complex sentences • Persuasive words • Suffixes – different endings with same pronunciation, e.g. '–tion', '–cian', '–ssion'	Fiction Writing a play script	Organization of ideas Expression of ideas Proverbs, sayings, figurative expressions Rehearsing a play script
• Connectives • Spelling patterns • Colons/semicolons	Non-fiction Persuasive writing Writing a speech	Expression of ideas
• Spelling patterns • Sentence length and structure • Word classes • Homophones	Non-fiction Writing a travel journal: Autobiography	Expressing opinions
• Speech punctuation • Apostrophes • Word origins • Borrowed words • Word classes • Active and passive verbs	Fiction Writing an extended narrative	Spoken presentation Kennings
• Specialized non-fiction vocabulary • Word classes • Relative clauses • Dashes and brackets • Speech punctuation	Fiction Writing a character description Writing a story starter	Poetry performance
• Language conventions • Grammatical features of different text types • Spelling: consonant choices for 'k' • Prefixes and suffixes • Spellings of unstressed vowels • Choosing appropriate adjectives	Non-fiction Writing a personal travel recount	Expression and explanation of ideas Language choices
• Spelling patterns • Connectives • Prefixes and suffixes • Commas in complex sentences	Non-fiction Writing a letter, presenting arguments for and against	Organization of ideas Expressing preferences
• Proverbs, sayings, figurative expressions • Conventions of standard English • Spelling patterns • Homophones • Connectives	Non-fiction Writing instructions	Organization of ideas Expressing opinions
• Word origins and derivations • Word changes over time • Language conventions • Grammatical features of different text types • Punctuation in persuasive texts: colon/semicolon, parenthetic commas, dashes, brackets	Non-fiction Writing interview questions	Organization of ideas Poetry performance
• Apostrophes • Speech punctuation • Word classes • Active and passive verbs	Non-fiction Writing an information leaflet	Organization of ideas Asking and answering questions Role play

1 We can all be heroes

These children organized a real-life campaign against nuclear power stations. They protested using placards. Many people saw the newspaper picture and understood their message.

In the film *Africa United*, these children followed their dream and walked 4,800 km to the football World Cup in South Africa from Rwanda. They looked after each other through thick and thin. They were local heroes when they went home to Rwanda.

Fabrice: "Do you know how big Africa is? It's impossible."
Dudu: "Impossible is nothing. Anything is possible."

Africa United

Let's Talk

1 Who are your local and national heroes? What did they do?

2 Have you worked together in a team to help others?

3 List three advantages of working together as a team on a project.

"Gira ubuntu!"

Learning objective

Express and explain ideas clearly, making meaning explicit.

Explore proverbs, sayings and figurative expressions.

Word Cloud

campaign
hero
protest
united

It feels good when we help other people, both friends and people we don't know, even if we only do something small. You could start a campaign at school and work together for a good cause. Your friends and families might support you.

"Ubuntu" is a Bantu word in Rwanda and in South Africa. It means that "I am what I am because of who we all are".

We can't be human by ourselves. We are all connected and united. The children in the *Africa United* story felt "ubuntu" because they stayed together through thick and thin and helped each other. We need to be kind and generous to others. "Gira ubuntu!" means "Be kind to others".

Gira ubuntu!

Glossary

a good cause a project that is worth supporting

through thick and thin in good times and bad times

A

You can be a hero by…

▶ taking care of your friends in trouble.

▶ helping your family.

▶ looking after the environment and getting others to join you.

Think of three more ways to be a hero.

B

Find these words on the first two pages of this unit. Use each one in a sentence of your own.

campaign   placards   protested   united

C

Are there any words in your language which mean the same as "Gira ubuntu!"? Explain them to the class.

Reefs at risk

Learning objective
Begin to develop awareness that the context for which the writer is writing and the context in which the reader is reading can impact on how the text is understood.

Word Cloud

courage	reef
damage	scallops
flippers	seal
lens	trawler

Kara saves an injured dolphin, then starts a campaign to protect the nearby reef from damage by overfishing. Kara's mother made a film about the reef before she died. The film is shown to the public and Kara finds the courage to stand up in front of all the townspeople to say what she believes.

Kara makes the people listen

"Dougie Evans is right," I say. My voice comes out much louder than I expect. The hall is silent, listening. "Fishing *is* the heart of this town." I look around. This is my one big chance.

5   "The boat my mum and dad rebuilt together, fished from this harbour a hundred years ago. Back then, she would have come home full of pilchard and herring, so full the fish would have been spilling over her sides into the sea." I swallow hard. The back of my throat is dry, like sawdust. I look around and fix my eye on Dougie Evans. "But she can't do that anymore. We've taken all the fish from our seas.

10 Dougie Evans's trawlers have to go further and deeper to find fish, and even then they sometimes come back empty. Now we're dredging our bay for scallops, tearing up the reef. I wonder, will we still be fishing here at all in another hundred years?" I glance across the hall. There's no sign of Felix, but I remember what he wanted me to say. "You're

15 about to see what we could lose."

    I stand there in the silence and look around the hall. I don't know what's meant to happen now. I climb down the steps and sit next to Dad.

    The hall lights go out.

20   I hear mum, speaking through the darkness.

    The room is silent. The huge screen on the stage is dark at first. A faint greenish glow in the centre of the screen becomes brighter and brighter and we are rising up, towards the sun shining through the surface of the water. A seal swims up to the

25 camera, his nose almost touching the lens. It's as if he's watching everyone in the hall. His big dog eyes are chocolate brown. He snorts a breath. Silver bubbles spiral upwards and he twists away, flippers pressed together, his grey body sliding through the water. And we're

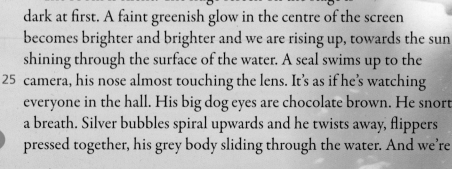

twisting through the water too: down, down, down through shafts of
10 rippling sunlight, past rocks jewelled with pink and green anemones,
down past coral mounds and feather-stars and sea-fans.

This must have been the last film mum made here in the bay...

But suddenly, a tearing sound rips through the hall. The image on
the screen changes and fills with metal chains and billowing mud and
15 sand. When the mud settles all that's left is a gravelly sea bed, littered
with broken sea-fans. The silence in the hall is still and deep.

Mum's voice speaks out one last time.

"Unless we protect our oceans, there will be nothing left
but wasteland. We are not farmers of the sea. We never sow, we
20 only reap."

The lights come on. No one speaks... A ripple of applause starts at
the back of the room and rolls forward like a wave. I look across to
see some of the fishermen nodding. Others are just staring at the
screen, transfixed.

From *White Dolphin* by Gill Lewis

Glossary

anemones sea creatures that look like flowers

coral colourful living creatures which grow into reefs after many years

dredge/dredging to drag something heavy along the bottom of the sea to scoop things up

herring an oily fish about 30cm long

pilchard young herring

sea-fans fan-shaped sea creatures

Comprehension

A

Give evidence from the text to support your answers.

1 Why are there no fish left?
2 What makes the sound and damages the sea-bed?
3 Which phrases in the text indicate that the seabed is being damaged by fishing?

B

What do you think?

1 What do you think will happen in the future unless changes are made to the present fishing methods?
2 What does the phrase in line 39, "We are not farmers of the sea. We never sow, we only reap." mean in the context of this story?
3 What does the writer want the reader to feel about sea damage?

C

What about you?

"You're about to see what we could lose," said Felix. What is there in your local environment that **you** could lose?

This reef has been damaged by a fisherman's anchor.

Sentence length in fiction texts

Learning objective

Begin to show awareness of writer's choices of sentence length and structure.

A

In the text extract from **White Dolphin** by Gill Lewis, the writer uses short sentences for dramatic effect. Look at the short sentences underlined below.

<u>The lights come on. No one speaks</u>. A ripple of applause starts at the back of the room and rolls forward like a wave. I look across to see some of the fishermen nodding. <u>Others are just staring at the screen</u>.

1 Join all the (short and long) sentences into one huge 'sentence', using 'and' to join each one.

2 What is the effect of 'losing' the short sentences?

Top Tips

▶ When you use 'and' consider whether you need to start a new sentence instead and get rid of the 'and'.

▶ Vary sentence length in your writing, so that there are both long and short sentences.

B

Look at the text below. The student has used too many 'ands' in their writing. Rewrite it so that these are taken out and a new sentence started instead. You will find that it is a much better piece of writing, with some very effective short sentences. (Note: A single 'and' should remain in the re-written text.)

It all started when I arrived home and I could see that the front door had been left open, so I felt a bit frightened and I wondered whether someone had broken in, so I opened the door very carefully and I tiptoed in and at first and I couldn't see anything, so I breathed a huge sigh of relief and suddenly, I heard a noise and a scream and I wanted to run for my life, but I knew I had to investigate and slowly, I made my way to the living room and I opened the door very, very gently and I saw my mother with a broken television at her feet and she had bought a new television, brought it in herself and, as it was too heavy, had dropped it and she had been so busy struggling with all of this that she hadn't managed to close the door and there hadn't been a burglar after all!

C

Write a 10-sentence account of travelling home to your house late at night. Use at least five very short sentences for dramatic effect.

Main and subordinate clauses

Learning objective
Develop grammatical control of complex sentences,
manipulating them for effect.

I like you when you are in a good mood.

A complex sentence consists of a **main clause** and one or more
subordinate clauses. A subordinate clause cannot stand alone, and
is usually introduced by a **subordinate connective** such as: who,
what, that, why, when, which, where, if, although, since, until, as.

Examples: I like you **when you are in a good mood**.
The weather, **which was really sunny**, meant everyone
went out.

A

Sometimes the subordinating connective is missed out. Here is a
sentence from *White Dolphin* by Gill Lewis:

'*I hear mum, speaking through the darkness.*'

This could have been written as 'I hear mum, who is speaking through
the darkness.'

**Rewrite the following sentences, missing out the subordinating
connective and making any necessary changes to the verb.**

1 I saw my friend <u>who was</u> running up the stairs.

2 The boy <u>who was</u> waiting in the room expected a phone call.

3 The house <u>that</u> stands at the end of the street will soon be sold.

B

Sometimes a present participle verb (ending in '–ing') or past
participle verb (ending in '–ed') can come at the beginning of a
sentence.

Example: Tired and depressed, I slumped on the sofa.

1 Start sentences with each of these participle verbs.

running walking laughing exhausted frightened

C

Subordinate clauses can be placed at different points in a sentence.

Example: Although Kara spoke clearly, they didn't listen. They didn't
listen although Kara spoke clearly.

1 Complete this sentence and put the clauses in different positions.

When I have free time I...

Word Cloud

extinct   habitat
generation   marine

Only 55 Maui's dolphins left in the world

Posted 13 March 2012

The World Wildlife Fund is urging people to support their campaign to protect Hector's and Maui's dolphins from extinction. Hector's dolphins are endangered, with about 7,000 remaining,
5 while Maui's dolphins are critically endangered, with only about 55 individuals left. Hector's and Maui's dolphins live round the shores of New Zealand and are among the rarest marine dolphins in the world, but unless urgent action is
10 taken, these amazing creatures could become extinct within a generation. But there is hope. By taking the necessary action and removing all human threats, New Zealand can give the dolphins their best chance of survival.

15 **Stop their extinction**
The biggest threat to Hector's and Maui's dolphins is from commercial and recreational fishing. The dolphins are unable to detect set nets – fixed nets that are held on or off shore with anchors – and, if
20 they become entangled, they drown in minutes. They are also accidentally caught by commercial fishing vessels. Add to this the disturbance to their natural habitat from tourism, polluted water, coastal development and boat traffic, and survival
25 for one of the world's rarest marine dolphins is a daily battle.

Supporting research studies
Scientists have been studying Maui's dolphins for over 20 years, but some questions remain
30 unanswered. For example, where do they live during the winter months? And how many of these tiny mammals are left?

A Maui's dolphin

New Zealand

Involving schools
Young New Zealanders have become fully
35 involved in the WWF campaign, for example, sending e-cards to ask for full protection for the dolphins. Students of Te Huruhi Primary School produced a short film with WWF-New Zealand Take Action for Maui's showing how involved they
40 are in the conservation project.

Working with Government
WWF-New Zealand has asked the Government to:

- regulate fishing to protect Maui's and Hector's dolphins
45 - produce an action plan that will lead to increased dolphin numbers

- support scientific research.

If everybody supports the WWF campaign, including the Government and the fishing
50 industry, these rare dolphins can be saved for future generations.

Comprehension

Learning objective

Help to move group discussion forward, by clarifying and summarizing.

A

Use the text to help you answer the questions.

1 What is the purpose of the campaign?

2 What are the different threats to the dolphins?

3 Why has the writer used a sentence beginning with 'if' in the final phrase?

B

What do you think?

1 As well as getting a petition together, what other actions could WWF take to save the dolphins?

2 Which phrases in the text indicate that the writer is confident of success?

C

What about you?

Which group or people in your country are carrying out good deeds for the protection of the environment? What are they doing?

> Bottle-nosed dolphins can die if trapped by fishing nets

Glossary

anchor a heavy metal weight that you drop into the water from a boat to stop the boat moving away

commercial connected with buying and selling things

detect to notice something that is difficult to see

entangled to become caught in a rope, net, etc.

recreational for relaxation and enjoyment

vessels boats

WWF (World Wildlife Fund) the world's leading independent conservation organization

Discussion time
In a small group, choose and plan a campaign for a real cause. Decide your action steps and then explain your plan to the rest of the class.

15

Persuasive words

 Learning objective
Explore definitions, shades of meaning and use of new words in context.

Top Tip

Before you start a piece of persuasive writing, collect some emotive words that you can use to convince your reader.

Writers use vocabulary that makes their meaning clear. In 'Maui's Dolphins', the writer chooses words and phrases to convince the reader that the Maui dolphins must be saved as soon as possible.

A

Find words in the extract which mean the same as:

Word from the extract	Dictionary definition
en_____	in danger of becoming extinct
_____al	continuing to live in or after a difficult time
th_____	a person or thing that may damage or hurt somebody or something
pro_____n	safety or care for an animal in danger

B

In the website report on Maui's dolphins, the writer uses emotive language – words which can have an emotional or dramatic effect on the reader.

Find emotive or dramatic words and phrases in the sentences below:

▶ ...among the rarest marine dolphins in the world, but unless urgent action is taken, these amazing creatures could become extinct within a generation.

▶ But there is hope.

▶ ...if they become entangled, they drown in minutes.

▶ ...survival for one of the world's rarest marine dolphins is a daily battle.

C

You have been asked to write a paragraph for the local newspaper on an animal that is soon going to be extinct. You must convince readers that something needs to be done.

Use the following words:

rarest   battle   extinct   survival   urgency   action   best hope   difference   future   generations   now

Suffixes

Learning objective
Learn words with different endings but the same pronunciation
e.g. –tion, –cian, –ssion.

Words that end in **–tion**, **–cian**, **–ssion** all make the same 'shun' sound in spite of their different spellings. The exercises below help to show which spelling to use.

A

Using a dictionary, find as many words as you can to add to the different word endings for 'shun' below.

–cian	– sion	–ssion	–tion
dietician	comprehension	discussion	attention
electrician	expansion	session	direction
magician	extension	passion	fiction
–otion	**–ution**	**–ition**	**–ation**
devotion	pollution	completion	demonstration
emotion	revolution	position	education
lotion	institution	repetition	station

B

Match the right ending to the right rule.

1 –cian

2 –tion   A   used where the base word ends in –ss

             B   used where the base word ends in –t

3 –ssion   C   used for jobs

C

Write a short humorous poem where you use the 'shun' sound at the end of each line. *Example:*

   I receive my education

   In this institution...

The poem can be about anything. The main objective is to use as many 'shun' words as you can!

An epic trip

> **Learning objective**
> Develop awareness of context for both the writer and reader of a text.

This is part of the film script from *Africa United*, the fictional story of the Rwandan children who walk 4,800 kilometres to the World Cup in South Africa using a World Cup wall chart as a map. Fabrice was spotted by a football talent scout and is determined to get there. Accompanied by Dudu, who decides to be his manager, and various friends, they make a dangerous journey through seven African countries with joy, laughter and hope, the "ubuntu" that comes from taking on a challenge together.

Africa United

BEATRICE: I've never seen the sea before. (*She stares out at a huge lake in wonder.*)

DUDU: Is that America?

FABRICE: It's Rwanda.

FOREMAN GEORGE: Burundi. This is Lake Tanganyika.
(*DUDU opens up his attaché case. He pulls out his World Cup wall chart, opens it up on the sand.*)

FABRICE: Burundi?

DUDU: They didn't qualify. They don't even have a team.
(*He puts a thumb on Burundi and stretches his fingers to South Africa. DUDU holds up thumb and index finger. FABRICE slaps his forehead.*)

FABRICE: Do you know how big Africa is? It's impossible.

DUDU: Impossible is nothing.
(*Holding up thumb and forefinger to prove it*).
Fabby, we can make it to the opening. Let's keep this dream alive and kicking like a donkey.

FABRICE: (*FABRICE stares out across the lake towards the north. Then he looks south towards the hills of Burundi on the far side.*)
My mother...

DUDU: Eh. The next time she sees you, you'll be in a stadium doing your silky skills in front of Mr and Mrs Obama and an audience of fifty hundred thousand... they'll be as proud as parrots.

FABRICE: (*FABRICE pictures it. It's a good picture but it's a picture he doesn't quite believe.*)
I've got exams.
(*Everyone jumps as FABRICE's phone gets a signal...*)
Signal!
(*FABRICE looks at his phone. He scrolls: 'missed call, missed call, missed call', then a text: 'Where are you?'*)

Word Cloud
attaché
tactical
winces

Dudu:	Who is it?
Fabrice:	Mum. What do I say?
Dudu:	Tell her... you got into the team for the dream and you need to go through more medicals, emotionals and tacticals.
Fabrice:	*(Fabrice thinks.)* She doesn't even know I went to the trial, Dudu...
Dudu:	Oh... this is double bubble trouble.
Fabrice:	*(Fabrice shakes his head. He starts to text: 'All fine. Don't worry.' He sends it and winces at the thought of it. The phone rings.)* What do I do?
Dudu:	Don't speak. She will only tell you that you can't go to the World Cup.
Fabrice:	*(Fabrice agonises as it RINGS and RINGS...)* I have to answer it.
Helene (Mum):	Fabrice, what's going on? You went to a football trial?
Fabrice:	Yes...
Helene (Mum):	What are you doing?
Fabrice:	We're... going... to the World Cup.
Helene (Mum):	Don't you sass me, boy. Tell me right now where you are and we will come and get you.
Fabrice:	No... *(Fabrice stands up.)*
Helene (Mum):	Fabrice, let me state this very clearly for you. You are not going to the World Cup.

Rehearsing a play script

Learning objective

Convey ideas about characters in drama through deliberate speech, gesture and movement.

Glossary

directions the instructions to the actors in a film or play

play script the text for actors in a film or play

A

Rehearse and act

1 Make groups of five. Take the parts of BEATRICE, FOREMAN GEORGE, FABRICE, DUDU and HELENE (MUM).

2 Read the play script through. Think about how to manage the directions as actors.

3 In your groups, practise reading the script aloud. You might need to add in some extra lines and more directions.

19

Write a playscript

Learning objective
Adapt the conventions of the text type for a particular purpose.

Storyline 1

An old lady has fallen over on the pavement and is unconscious. A and B go to help her.

Storyline 2

A child has fallen off her bike and has broken her arm. A and B go to help her.

Storyline 3

Two bullies have stolen a boy's bag. A and B go to help him.

An accident

A

Look back at the extract on pages 18 and 19 and find these examples of features of a play script.

a The speaker's name, written in the left-hand margin

b The directions in italics

c Present tense in the directions

d Character names in the directions, written in capital letters

e Directions are written in sentences so need capital letters and full stops.

B

1 Write your own playscript and directions, using one of the storylines on page 20.

2 Give the characters in the story names.

3 As you are writing your play script, put your directions in brackets instead of using italics. *Example storyline 1:*

LUCA   (*LUCA pulls ENZO by the sleeve.*)
         Look! That old woman's fallen over. I think she's hurt herself.

ENZO   (*ENZO looks towards the woman on the pavement.*)
         She's not moving. I think she's unconscious.

4 Choose from some of these phrases below to help you as you write your play script.

> *Examples:*
>
> 1 **To describe what's just happened**
>
>   X has been knocked off her bike / had his bag stolen / fallen over
>
> 2 **To describe what is happening**
>
>   The boys are running off / She is lying very still / Her shopping is flying everywhere
>
> 3 **To describe injuries or danger**
>
>   I think he's crying / She's unconscious / She's in pain
>
> 4 **To suggest actions**
>
>   We must go and get help / ring for an ambulance / talk to him
>
>   We shouldn't move her / give her anything to drink

Top Tips

- Read out your dialogue in pairs, to check it sounds natural and the way people really speak.

- Directions tell actors to show exact feelings.

- Directions tell a character when and where to move.

- There are no speech marks in play scripts.

2 Health and sport

Sachin Tendulkar batting for India

Saudi women's tea

New Zealand player Lydia Ko, aged 15

Fiji playing against Samoa

Let's Talk

1 Name the sport in each picture.

2 Is it more important to win a sporting event, or to just take part?

3 What are the most popular sports in your country?

"Obstacles don't have to stop you... don't give up."
Michael Jordan

Are you fit and healthy?

Learning objective
Express and explain ideas, making meaning clear.

Word Cloud

exercise   physical
free time   sports day
fried

Health Quiz

1 **How often do you have a sports lesson or physical activity in school?**
   a) once or twice a week or less
   b) more than twice a week   c) every day

2 **How often do you walk or cycle to school?**
   a) never   b) sometimes   c) most days

3 **In your free time, how often do you do physical exercise?** a) never
   b) once or twice a week   c) more than twice a week

4 **There's a sports day in your school. Do you usually:**
   a) not take part   b) sign up for your favourite and best event   c) sign up for all the events?

5 **At lunch do you eat:**
   a) chocolate and sweets   b) not very much as you'd rather play outside   c) fresh fruit and vegetables

Answer Key
C answers = 5 points each   **B** answers = 3 points each
A answers = 1 point each
Over 20 points: Well done! You are really fit!
Over 15 points: You are on the right road! Keep going!
Less than 15 points: Exercise and healthy food are good for you. Try to do more exercise and eat more healthily!

··· Challenge ···

Tell a partner about a sport or activity *you* have done over the last week. Don't use the word '**and**', not even once.
Example: On Monday, I walked two miles to school. Then I sat in lessons till break. At break I played basketball.

Compare your answers with a friend's and check your score using the answer key.

Alaskan adventure

Learning objective
Analyze the success of writing in evoking particular moods.

A young Alaska native girl, Bright Dawn, takes her father's place in a gruelling dogsled race that covers 1600 kilometres. Running with ears laid back and nose in the air Black Star, leader of her dog team, guides them through dangers on the race trail.

Word Cloud

billowing	ragged
dazed	runners
gruelling	scooped
handlebar	seized
lagoon	

The Iditarod Great Sled Race

The country beyond looked wild and forsaken. Scattered trees were ragged and bent over by fierce winds. It was very cold. My feet stuck to the [sled] runners. They felt as if they belonged to somebody else.

I drove the team faster than I ever had before. At times we were
5 running at fifteen miles an hour. The dogs opened their jaws and scooped up snow as they ran...

The trail wound through steep hills and the temperature was now much below zero. My eyelashes gathered frost and began to feel like splinters. I had a hard time seeing and had to depend on Black Star.

10 I was travelling on a lagoon formed by the Innoko River, when the trail began to tremble. At once I realized that we were on ice, thin ice, no more than a couple of inches thick. Ahead of us it was billowing like waves on the sea.

Black Star saw the billows too and stopped the dogs. If we went
15 on, the whole team, all of us, would go crashing down into the rushing river. We were trapped. Panic seized me. Black Star stood with his ears curled back tight against his head. He was trying to decide where to go, to the right or to the left. I was of no help. It was Black Star's decision.

20 At last he turned toward a line of trees that marked the shore. He went slowly and the team followed him.

The ice grew thinner. It creaked beneath the weight of the sled. Through the ice I could see fish swimming and blue water racing over the rocks. Black Star's head was up and his ears alert, his bushy tail
25 curved high over his back. The rest of the team were dragging their tails. Suddenly Black Star pulled up. Then, slowly gathering speed, with the bank only a few yards away, he made a dash and scrambled safely to shore. The next five dogs followed him. Then the ice broke and the rest of the team fell through
30 into the swirling water. The sled went with them and I went with the sled.

The map labels read: Nome, ALASKA, Anchorage, ALASKA, CANADA, USA.

Dazed and blinded, I held tight to the sled handlebar. The dogs were struggling against the current, their heads up and silent. There was a gray mist among the trees, but I had a glimpse of my leader. He and his five dogs were pulling on the towline. With all my strength I shouted, "Go, Black Star, go!"

From *Black Star, Bright Dawn* by Scott O'Dell

Glossary

Alaska native a general term for the range of different indigenous people of Alaska

forsaken to forsake someone is to abandon them

panic to panic is to be overcome with fear or anxiety and behave wildly

splinter a small sharp piece of wood or glass broken off a larger piece

Comprehension

A

Use words and phrases from the text to support your answers.

1 Number these statements 1–3 so that they are in the right order.

Black Star and five dogs make it to the shore.

Bright Dawn and some dogs crash through the ice.

Bright Dawn and the dog team are travelling very fast.

2 Find one sentence or phrase which shows that Bright Dawn treats Black Star as the leader.

3 Read lines 30–36 again. What evidence is there that Bright Dawn and the dogs will be pulled to safety?

B

Writer's use of language

1 Find three phrases which show the race takes place in harsh conditions.

2 The writer uses short sentences. What mood does this create?

3 Choose six verbs from the extract to show the writer has created a mood of tension and movement.

The person in charge of the dogsled is called a musher or driver.

C

What about you?

With a partner, write a paragraph from the dog Black Star's point of view – as if he were telling the story, with excitement and tension, about the race.

Colons and semicolons

Learning objective
Identify uses of the colon and semicolon.

A **colon** : is a punctuation mark that acts as a sign to the reader that something is coming, such as a list.

Example:
The following students from Grade six have been selected for the school football team: Ali Yavuz, Juan Lopez, JuYoung Kim, Martin Andres and Oleg Hof.

The first word after the colon will only have a capital letter if it is a proper noun.

A

Write the sentences out, putting the colons in the correct place.

1 I have lived in many cities San Francisco, Rome, Sydney, Dubai, New Delhi and London.

2 The plan you have suggested has three advantages it is cheap, it is sensible and it will be popular.

3 Roald Dahl is the author of *Charlie and the Chocolate Factory*, *James and the Giant Peach*, *The BFG* and *The Twits*.

A **semicolon** ; can be used to separate longer phrases in a list. Commas could be used, but using a semicolon makes the sentence clearer.

Example:
Yesterday, I bought the following items: two bunches of large, ripe bananas; six large, fresh bread rolls; two small T-shirts; four juicy peaches; and eight boxes of tea.

B

Items on Bright Dawn's sled are shown on the right. Write a sentence listing the items. Correctly use a colon before the list starts and semicolons **in-between the items**.

Using colons and semicolons

Learning objective
Practise using colons and semicolons in a range of sentences.

A semicolon can be used instead of **and** or **but** to join two related sentences into one sentence.

Examples:
The boy burst through the door. He glared at me.
The boy burst through the door **and** (he) glared at me.
The boy burst through the door**;** he glared at me.

A

Match the sentences below using a semicolon to join them up.

Example: Fruit is good for you; burgers are not.

I listened to the gentle patter of rain against the window	he likes tennis
The plates are in the cupboard	I love rain
She loves playing football	the spoons are in the drawer

B

Add semicolons to the sentences below. They could be used to separate items in a list or replace 'and' or 'but'.

1 Football is a game for young people many older people prefer golf.

2 I prefer reading she likes dancing.

3 We were told to bring the following equipment to the sports class our basketball kit and boots a large towel snacks water bottle and money.

4 The students ran home they shouted all the way.

A pair of old walking boots

A mobile phone

A large red apple

A bottle of water

A fur hat

Half a chocolate bar

A notebook

A first aid kit

A sleeping bag

Wheelchair athlete

Learning objective
Recognize key text features of journalistic interviews.

Word Cloud
backflip   spine
category   stunts
ramp

We Salute You!

Aaron Fotheringham, known as 'Wheelz', is a pioneer in the sport of wheelchair motocross (WCMX). He is a wheelchair athlete. Aaron performs tricks and stunts in his wheelchair all over the world. At the age of 14, he successfully performed the first ever backflip in a wheelchair. Born on 8 November 1991 in Las Vegas, Nevada, USA, he has been a wheelchair user since the age of eight. Aaron has a birth defect called Spina Bifida which affects the spine and central nervous system.

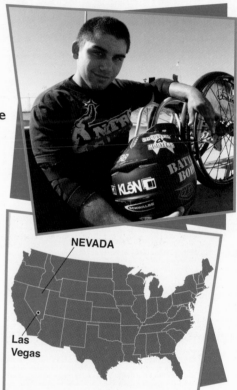

NEVADA

Las Vegas

What is wheelchair motocross?
WCMX is a term that I thought up for extreme wheelchairing in skateparks. It's adapting existing skateboard and BMX (bike) moves for a wheelchair and making up new moves only a wheelchair can do.

How and when did you start this extreme sport?
My older brother, Brian, used to BMX and so he inspired me to start riding in skateparks. That was back in 2000.

How does it make you feel?
It makes me feel like I'm alive and not just playing video games.

What do you find hardest?
Coming up with new tricks is the hardest thing I've found.
And then after you come up with the trick, you actually have to land it!

How much time do you spend practising during each session?
It depends on the weather, but it can range from 2–8 hours.

What is your favourite trick?
The handplant. This is where you go up the quarter pipe (a curved, sloped ramp) and stall (balance) on one hand.

How did you feel when you did your first record breaking backflip?
I was speechless! It was amazing. After all my hard work, I got my reward.

Are there any tricks that you haven't been able to do yet?
It's not that I'm not able, it's just that I can't find a big enough ramp to be able to do them on!

Where would you like to see your sport go in the future?
I want to see it as a category in X Games (X Games is an extreme sports competition that is held every year in summer and winter).

Comprehension

Learning objective

Recognize key text features of journalistic interviews.

Glossary

central nervous system the system, consisting of the brain, spinal cord, and nerves, which sends electrical messages from one part of the body to another

pioneer one of the first people to go to a place or do something new

skateparks places where people can skate

A

Explain your answers using words and phrases from the text.

1 Why does Aaron use a wheelchair?

2 How do you know that Aaron is a very determined person?

3 How old is Aaron now?

B

What do you think?

1 Interviewers need to use the right type of question words. Write down three from the text and add three more that start with 'wh'.

2 Why does the interviewer sometimes ask 'fact' questions and sometimes 'feeling' questions?

3 Which type of questions help the reader to understand the sport?

4 Why does the interviewer put the question about the future at the end?

C

What about you?

1 Write four more questions you would like to ask Aaron.

2 Which sports person would you like to interview?

3 Research your favourite sports person and prepare an interview for them which will take place on national TV or radio. Write out your questions using good interview techniques.

Discussion time

What could be done within your own community to encourage everyone, even those with a physical disability, to get involved in sport?

Connectives

Learning objective
Investigate meanings and spellings of connectives.

When you want to explain points to a reader (or persuade them!), it is important to help them follow your ideas. There are different categories of **connective** words and phrases to help you do this.

▶ **Connectives are used to add points.**

Examples:
Also   Furthermore   In addition   For example   Moreover

▶ **Connectives are used to change the topic or suggest a different view.**

Examples:
However   On the other hand   Yet   Although

▶ **Connectives help to put points in order.**

Examples:
First of all   Secondly   Next   After that   Eventually   Finally

▶ **Connectives help to explain a point in more detail.**

Examples:
For example   This means that   This shows   Therefore   Similarly

A

Add another sentence to each of the sentences below using one connective from each of the above categories.

Example:

I prefer team sports. **However**, my sister likes individual sports best.

1 I prefer team sports.

2 Some people think that young people do not do enough sport.

3 Swimming increases fitness.

4 Sports require skill and team work.

Spelling connectives

Learning objective
Continue to learn words, apply patterns, and improve accuracy in spelling.

Connectives are very helpful if you want to show a sequence of ideas or actions.
Example: **First**, you need to ensure you want to get fit. **Second**, you need to find out about some suitable exercises. **Next**, you need to tell everyone that you are going to get fit, as that will make you do it. **Finally**, you just need to get going!

A

1 Explain how to play or do a particular sport, using connectives to put the steps in order so that they are easy to understand.

2 Highlight or underline the connectives.

3 Read your sport instructions to a partner, but say the connectives loudly, so that they are really emphasized.

These strategies will help you remember the spelling of connectives.

Break them into chunks or syllables.

Examples: there/fore; more/over

Find words within words.

Examples: **how**ever, **more**over, **there**fore

Highlight tricky bits or letters.

Examples: **al**though, **add**ition

Discussion time
'Everyone should be free to choose how much to exercise and to eat junk food if they want to.'
Discuss why you agree or disagree. Use connectives to order your points and ideas.

B

1 Collect more connectives for each of the different categories and write them in your notebook.

2 Write down some different strategies for remembering the spellings.

Modern rhyming poem

Learning objective
Explore how poets manipulate and play with words and their sounds.

Word Cloud

chasm   salute
endurance   setbacks
gain   unyielding
leap

Brian Moses is a famous children's poet who has performed in over two thousand schools. He began writing poems when he realized he would never be a rock star.

Salute

The chasm is so much wider,
the fall is so much tougher,
the challenge so much greater,
4   the road ahead much rougher.

The training much more exhausting,
the setbacks much harder to take,
the path ahead unyielding
8   the leap more difficult to make.

So much stamina needed,
so much bravery overcoming pain,
so much strength, so much endurance,
12   so fantastic to make each gain.

The widest skies in the world
would still not limit their dream.
Everyone, please salute
16   our Paralympic team.

Brian Moses

Zahra Nemati winner of a gold medal in Archery at the 2012 Paralympics.

Comprehension

A

Give evidence from the poem to support answers to A and B.

1 The poet has called the poem 'Salute'. Which statement below explains the reason for the poem's title?

   a To express admiration for the courage and determination of the paralympic team.

   b To show that the paralympic team normally salute at the end of a sporting event.

   c To ask the readers to salute at the end of the poem.

2 Name three qualities a paralympic athlete needs.

3 The paralympic athlete has to put in great effort. Which two words emphasize this throughout the poem?

4 Which sentence explains that the athlete will not stop competing?

B

Poet's use of language

1 Look again at the first three verses. What do you notice about how each line starts?

2 The poet uses rhyme at the end of some lines to emphasize his feelings and create a rhythm. Write down the rhyming word pairs.

3 The poet refers to 'our Paralympic team'. Which word class is 'our'?

   a pronoun

   b adjective

   c preposition

4 Why has the poet used the word 'our' and not 'the'?

C

What about you?

Tell a partner about the most challenging situation you have been in.

It could be:

▶ moving to a new school or country.

▶ taking part in a competition or an exam.

▶ helping to care for a sick family member.

Listen to each other, and then ask and answer these questions:

a How did you overcome the difficulties?

b What advice would you give to someone facing the same challenge?

Tanni Grey Thompson, paralympic athlete

'88 SEOUL PARALYMPICS

The logo of the first ever Paralympic games

Writing to persuade

Learning objective
Argue a case in writing, developing points logically and convincingly.

Top Tip

Persuasive writing has:
Short sentences
Rhetorical questions
Sets of three words or phrases
Emotive words

You are a member of the student council. You have been asked to write a speech to present to the school Principal requesting more time for sport at your school.

Your aim is to persuade the Principal to accept and agree with your point of view.

Getting the right start

The first paragraph of an argument should tell the Principal what your argument is about and what you hope to achieve. This makes it very clear to them at the beginning exactly what they can expect! Read these two introductory paragraphs below. Which paragraph gets the argument off to the best start?

STUDENT A

Good morning, Principal. My name is Jacintha Dolores, and I am here today to try to persuade you to let us have more time in school for sporting activities. At present, we only have one hour a week. We think it should be increased to at least two hours a week. Here are the reasons for our request.

Correct formal address, ' Good morning, Principal. My name is...'

Says WHY they are writing, summing up what the argument is. Does not go on to the reasons yet.

Gives a clear link to the next paragraph, 'Here are the reasons for'.

STUDENT B

Hi! We're getting fed up not having sport. Everyone wants more because sport keeps you fit and healthy and it also gives you other qualities like determination. So why can't we have more time? I want to hear back from you.

Informal address, 'Hi!'

Does not sum up what the argument is or why they are writing.

No link to the next paragraph.

Whole argument covered in one paragraph!

Developing your argument

It is important that each paragraph covers only one point. Usually, you state what the paragraph is going to be about through a topic sentence.

Example:
Firstly, more sport will mean that children will be fitter and healthier.

Then you go on to prove it. You can prove your topic sentence by giving:

a Examples

b Facts and statistics

c A personal anecdote (a personal 'story' of someone you know or have heard about)

d Finishing it with a sentence that contrasts how things are now and how they could be in the future.

Find examples of **a, b, c,** and **d** in the second paragraph written by Student A.

> First, more time given to sport will mean that children will be fitter and healthier. At present, they have one hour of sport a week. That is simply not enough. Government research shows that if children have the minimum exercise of two hours a week, their fitness rates will go up by 40%. Surely you want this for the children in your school? I have a close friend who is overweight and unfit, and actually begged the Head of Physical education for more time on sport because he desperately wants to become fitter. The choice is yours, sir. Fitter, healthier, happier children who enjoy two hours of sport a week — or unhealthy unfit children who have barely enough time to enjoy one sporting slot over a whole week.

Summing up

A good conclusion will refer back to the beginning and sum up the argument:

> I trust I have made a convincing argument for having two hours a week of sport in the school rather than one hour. The children in this school will be fitter, healthier, happier, and, most importantly, more ready and willing to learn. Thank you for your time and attention.

Write your own speech to your Principal, arguing for more time for sports activities. Use as many of the following techniques as you can:

▶ A clear introduction stating your argument and what you hope to achieve. Build up your argument step by step, in each paragraph.

▶ Have a clear topic sentence for each paragraph, which you then prove using:

    a Examples   **c** A personal anecdote

    b Facts and statistics   **d** Comparing the present to the future

▶ Some persuasive techniques, such as short sentences, rhetorical question, sets of three words and phrases, emotive vocabulary

▶ A conclusion which refers back to the beginning paragraph and sums up the argument

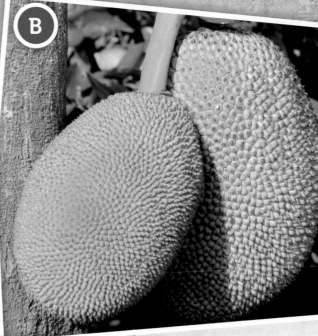

> "Judge a man by his questions rather than by his answers."
>
> Voltaire, 1694–1778

Let's Talk

1 Why do you think it is important to find out about our world and the past?

2 What would you like to find out about the world?

Discovering new things and new places

Learning objective
Continue to learn words, apply patterns and improve accuracy in spelling.

Word Cloud

adventure | explore
ancestor | medicinal
archaeologist | replica
botanist | rhinoceros
discover | scientist
expedition | willow

A

Match the sentences to the illustrations on these two pages.

Example: 1 = E

1 Hippocrates was an ancient Greek doctor who discovered that the bark and leaves of the willow tree cure headaches and fevers.

2 Artists who travelled with Joseph Banks, the botanist, drew pictures of plants like this breadfruit.

3 Joseph Banks and his friends sailed with Captain Cook on the *Endeavour* from 1769 to 1771. This replica is the same size and the mast is 9.39 metres high, the height of 24 men.

4 This drawing of a rhinoceros was made in 1515. Look carefully. Do you think that the artist had seen a rhinoceros?

5 This drawing shows that Mexicans collected medicinal plants.

6 Archaeologists are making exciting discoveries about a lost underwater city in Egypt.

B

These people all like to study and discover things. Talk about them together and match the words and explanations. Which one would you like to be?

archaeologist	studies the history and archaeology of Egypt
marine archaeologist	studies plants
zoologist	studies rocks
botanist	studies human evidence discovered underwater
geologist	studies animals and birds
Egyptologist	studies ancient history by examining what people leave behind them under the ground.
palaeontologist	studies fossils of animals and plants

The diary of a stowaway

Learning objective
Understand aspects of narrative structure, for example, the handling of time.

This is from the imaginary journal of a real boy, Nicholas Young, who was a stowaway on the ship *Endeavour*. He helped Joseph Banks on the ship and was given a job by him when they returned home. The 'Gentlemen' are Mr Banks, the scientists and artists. The author used Captain Cook's real journal to help her write this fictional journal.

Word Cloud

creatures   log
deck   planet
diary   presence
itch   stowaway
journal   voyage

The Start of a Great Adventure

Sunday 7th to Friday 19th August 1768 (Plymouth).
I have managed to keep my presence aboard *Endeavour* secret.
The three seamen I paid to get me on bring biscuits and water.
It's a good hiding place I've got, in the aft of the Pinnace, a
5 small boat *Endeavour* carries aboard her. I can look over the
edge and see the deck without being noticed. I've chickens for
neighbours, and a goat. They cluck and bleat all day and night,
in pens on deck. I'm glad of their company and wish I might
go near them more often. I've had milk out of the goat. John
10 Ramsay says she's aboard for the Gentlemen and officers, so
they might have fresh cream when they please...

Tuesday 23rd August (Plymouth). Last night the servant
boy came right to my hiding place.

"Lad," he whispered, "are you still alive in there?" I held
15 silent. After a moment he poked his head into the Pinnace and
stared straight at me. When he made out I was well, he smiled.
He dropped some hardtack into my hand...

Tuesday 6th September (Off the coast of Spain). Mr Parkinson and
Mr Buchan, the artists aboard, must be very busy men to draw all the
20 creatures Mr Banks discovers. Now his discoveries are all recorded in
Mr Parkinson's and Mr Buchan's pictures...

Thursday 8th September (Off the coast of Spain). John Ramsay
says, "We are pulling away from Cape Saint Vincent, lad, the last of
Europe. And soon you shall come out."

25 It's difficult deciding what to do first. A wash — what with the
fleas and a coat of saltwater on my skin, I itch like mad — or dinner.
I think it shall be dinner...

Glossary

aboard on a ship

hardtack hard bread, like a biscuit

journal a diary kept on a journey

pinnace a small boat, kept on a ship

Monday 12th September (Isle of Madeira). John Charlton checked on me. "We're heading from here to Brasil, Nick. Then round Cape Horn to King George's Land. We're to observe the Planet Venus whilst we're there. It's very important, this observation, Nick. Captain says it will tell us how far the Earth is from the Sun and help all men who go to sea ever after."

I only wanted a long voyage. I did not know I had stowed away on such an important one.

From *Stowaway* by Karen Hesse

Comprehension

A

Give evidence from the extract to support your answers.

1 Which two of the following statements are false?

   a Nicholas Young is not a real person.

   b He can't see anything from his hiding place.

   c Nobody knows he is on the ship.

   d He will come out of hiding when the ship leaves Spain.

2 Who are Nick's neighbours on deck and why are they there?

3 What are the scientists going to observe?

4 Find three phrases that show the seamen were kind to Nick.

A model replica of the *Endeavour* shows the small boat Pinnace on the deck

B

Writer's use of language

1 What structure has the author used to make the story easy to follow?

2 How many journal entries are there?

3 Why are some of the diary entries shorter than others?

4 Write down two phrases or sentences which refer to Nick's hiding, and the possibility that he might get out.

C

What about you?

1 How would you feel if you were on such a long voyage on a ship?

Eating area for crew on the ship *Endeavour*

Simple, compound and complex sentences

Learning objective
Begin to show awareness of the impact of writers' choices
of sentence length and structure.

Writers choose different types of sentences depending on what it is
they want to write. Long, complex sentences will link up information
and ideas. In a compound or simple sentence the information will
be more direct and to the point.

In the fiction extract, 'The Start of a Great Adventure', many simple
sentences have been used. A simple sentence has just one finite
verb. A finite verb is a verb that has a subject. *Example*:

He (subject) **dropped** (finite verb) some hardtack into my hand.

A

Pick out the finite verbs in each of these simple sentences.

I held silent.

They cluck and bleat all day and night.

John Charlton checked on me.

I only wanted a long voyage.

Last night the servant boy came right to my hiding place.

Compound sentences are two simple sentences joined by 'and', 'but'
or 'or'. This means that both clauses should have **two finite verbs**.

Complex sentences are required when the writer needs to explain
and link ideas.

B

1 Find one compound sentence in the extract, 'The Start of a Great
Adventure'.

2 Find four subordinate clauses which use each of these connectives.

So   Whilst   When   Who

C

Write six sentences describing what you have done so far today. Use:

1 two simple sentences

2 two compound sentences

3 two complex sentences

Modals

Learning objective
Revise different word classes.

Often verbs are 'helped' by 'auxiliary' verbs.

Example: I **have** done my homework.

An important group of auxiliary verbs are called **modals**. These include:

can/could   will/would   shall/should   may/might

must/ought

They are used to indicate how sure the writer is that something happened, is happening or will happen.

Examples:

It is raining, so it **must** be very wet outside.

I don't know where Nick is. He **may** have missed the boat.

I like adventure. I **might** travel the world in future.

A

Complete these sentences.

1 If I win a lot of money, I can…

2 If I was able to win a lot of money, I could…

3 If I was able to win a lot of money, I would…

4 If I was able to win a lot of money, I should…

5 If I win a lot of money, I ought…

B

Insert the missing modals in these sentences.

must   may   should   could   can

1 She _____ speak French and English.

2 I _____ go on holiday if I save enough money.

3 The school rules say that students _____ do their homework.

4 I really think that you _____ stop eating so much.

5 _____ I go to the film tonight?

C

Write three or four sentences which make excuses for not doing some housework. At least four modals should be used. You could start, 'I should have done it, but…'

Egypt's drowned cities

Learning objective
Analyse how paragraphs and chapters are structured and linked.

Word Cloud

ancient	jewellery
diver	statue
drowned	surface

Bringing the past to life

In 2000, the drowned cities of Herakleion and Canopus were discovered as well as the ancient harbour of Alexandria close to Egypt's Mediterranean coasts. Marine archaeologist
5 Franck Goddio, with a team of Egyptologists, historians, geologists, engineers and computer experts is still working there as there is so much to discover.

(Think of a title for this paragraph)

10 Marine archaeologists think that the towns existed 2500 years ago. They have found statues, sphinxes, pottery, jewellery and coins, less than 10 metres below sea-level. They also found a large stone which shows the position of
15 the towns. Herakleion and Canopus were important business and holy place centres even before the foundation of Alexandria, which is now on the Egyptian coast. Herakleion and Canopus were built on sandy, marshy ground which was
20 then near the sea.

(Think of a title for this paragraph)
Each dive is planned carefully. The divers know their way round the sunken cities like their home towns. Computers are used to make maps of the
25 streets and buildings as more is discovered. The marine archaeologists have even been able to find tiny treasures hidden in sand and mud. The biggest Egyptian statue ever found had slept underwater for over 2000 years and is over five
30 metres tall and weighs 6000 kilograms.

A long lost statue is brought to the surface.

(Think of a title for this paragraph)
Scientists think that the city was sent to the bottom of the sea after an earthquake and tsunami more than a thousand years ago. Geologists
35 know that there were many earthquakes in the Mediterranean and North Africa at that time. The old coast must have dropped about seven metres.

(Think of a title for this paragraph)
Most discoveries are being mapped and left
40 under the sea. But some special discoveries are on show to the public in a national museum. It will take many years to finish the work on this site as it is so big.

Glossary

sphinxes mythological creatures from Ancient Egypt. They had a human head and the body of a lion.

Comprehension

A

Large teams of experts are needed to investigate the drowned cities of Egypt. Use phrases from the text to complete the table below.

1

Expert	One piece of evidence from the text that shows what they do or have found
Marine archaeologist	
Computer expert	
Scientist	
Diver	

Discussion time
Which four everyday items would give a future archaeologists the best information on how we live today for example; computer, book, car, aeroplane. In a group give reasons for each of your choices.

2 The marine archaeologists

  a have finished work at Herakleion

  b will finish the work soon

  c will be there for many years.

B

What do you think?

1 What do you think is a good subheading for each paragraph? Write down your ideas.

2 The title `Bringing the past to life' is interesting because it is not really possible. The title makes the reader want to find out more. Suggest a different title for the text.

C

What about you?

1 Imagine that the underwater cities can now be visited using a special glass deep-sea boat. What would you want to see?

2 Find out about your nearest archaeological museum. With a partner explain why it would make a good place for a school trip.

Another exciting discovery from the lost city of Herakleion

Homophones

Learning objective
Continue to learn words, apply patterns and improve accuracy in spelling.

A homophone is a word which has the same sound as another, but a different spelling and a different meaning.

Examples: 'site' (place) and 'sight' (something seen)

'weighs' (how heavy) and 'ways' (means)

A

Using a dictionary to help you, write down the definitions of the following homophone pairs.

▶ allowed/aloud   ▶ meter/metre

▶ pair/pear   ▶ knew/new

▶ mail/male   ▶ piece/peace

▶ manner/manor   ▶ waste/waist

A pair of pears

B

Fill in the missing words.

1 The perfect leaving gift for the headteacher is good quality _____ (stationery/stationary)

2 It's the only _____ with 60% fruit! (cereal/serial)

3 The _____ has been appalling. (weather/whether)

4 _____ go to the cinema tonight. (let's/ lets)

5 Drivers should carry a current driving _____ . (licence/license)

C

Write a short letter to your mayor or town leader, complaining about the noise and danger caused by cars outside your school. Use all of the following words.

its   it's   quiet   quite   to   too
past   passed   allowed   aloud

Excellent adjectives!

Adjectives provide more information about a noun.

Example: **long-lost** statue of an **ancient Egyptian** king.

A

Find six more adjectives (and their nouns) in the non-fiction extract, 'Bringing the past to life'.

Adjectives can be added before the noun.

Example: the bedroom = the cold bedroom = the cold, damp bedroom.

B

Add two more adjectives before the following nouns. Remember the commas!

1   A _____ man
2   A _____ house
3   A _____ dog
4   A _____ school
5   A _____ door

Adjectives can also come after linking verbs, such as:

appear; be; become; feel; seem; look; turn.

Example: You look **nice**.

C

Correct the following sentences, so that adjectives are used not adverbs.

1   Maria seemed sadly.
2   John felt happily.
3   The milk went badly.

4   The train is slowly.
5   The sea turned roughly.
6   The cake tastes well.

45

A dialogue poem

Learning objective

Explore how poets manipulate and play with words and their sounds.

Bobbi Katz was born in New York State, USA. She trained as an art historian and is also a well-known poet. This poem is a dialogue between a geologist and an oceanographer. They are discussing what happened to an underwater city.

Word Cloud

cataclysm   marshland
deltas   oceanographer
earthquake   tectonic force
geologist   toppled
landslide   waterlogged

Herakleion: An Underwater City in the Bay of Abukir off the North Coast of Egypt

Dr Nur, Geologist

2 Did some cataclysm happen?

Or did the city slowly sink?

4 Did an underwater landslide

cause an earthquake,

6 as I think?

         Dr Stanley, Oceanographer

         8 *Herakleion stood on marshland,*

         waterlogged and almost mud.

         10 *While I don't rule out an earthquake,*

         I think there was a flood.

12   We know an earthquake

toppled Troy.

14 One toppled Jericho.

Perhaps there's a still-hidden fault

16 Just where, we still don't know.

         If there had been an earthquake,

         18 *It would seem to me*

         there would be a record,

         20 *but there's none that we can see.*

The temple has a long
    deep
    crack:
proof of tectonic force...

      26 *That crack is typical of deltas,*
          of large rivers
      28 *changing course...*

  What happened at Herakleion?
30 The jury may still be out.
  Asking questions, seeking answers...
32 That's what exploring's all about!

Bobbi Katz

Look at the pattern of this poem.

1 It has a dialogue, with alternate verses. It is like a conversation. Each person gives their opinion.

2 There is a third person, a narrator, who speaks the last verse.

Comprehension

A

1 Which of the two speakers argues that the underwater city was caused by an earthquake?

2 Which of the two speakers argues that the underwater city was caused by a flood?

Have you heard of the lost city of Atlantis? Could the legend of Atlantis be based on the underwater cities of Egypt?

B

What do you think?

1 What sentence type has been repeated in the first verse?

  a statement **b** imperative **c** exclamatory **d** interrogative

2 Which lines rhyme in verses 1, 2, 3 and 7?

3 Read verses 5 and 6 again. Which one word are the speakers arguing about?

4 Which line sums up what the whole poem is about?

  a Asking questions, seeking answers.

  b Did some cataclysm happen?

  c I think there was a flood.

C

What about you?

In pairs, write one four line verse each of a dialogue poem. Choose a topic that you disagree on such as sports or holidays.

Glossary

fault crack in the earth. Fault lines lie between the Earth's tectonic plates.

Jericho, Troy famous ancient cities. Jericho still exists.

tectonic from geology, it means 'connected to the Earth's surface'. The Earth's surface is covered by moving tectonic plates. When they collide, earthquakes result.

the jury may still be out people may not have reached a conclusion yet

Keeping a travel journal

Learning objective
Develop skills of writing biography and autobiography in role.

The original meaning of a journal is a diary about a journey. Today, it is more often used to mean a magazine. You can make your own travel journal. Use an ordinary notebook and decorate the cover to show where you have been.

Nicholas Young's journal was imaginary, but Joseph Banks wrote a real journal about all the plants and animals that he saw, and artists who travelled with him made drawings.

This illustration of a kanagaroo appeared in Joseph Banks' journal

An imaginary journey
You are going to write a journal of your trip. First you need to plan:

who you are going to be. You can be anybody on any kind of ship you like.

when the journey takes place

what kind of ship you are on
Examples: an oil tanker, a sailing ship, a cargo ship

where you are going

Plan your writing
Work out the details of your trip, using the questions below for guidance.

Who are you and how old are you?	
Where do you live?	
What year is it?	
What sort of ship do you want to go on?	
What is the reason for the ship's voyage?	
Are you a stowaway or not? If not, what are you?	
What do you do on the ship?	
Who are your friends?	
Where is the ship going?	
Who else is on the ship?	
How does the voyage end?	

Writing frame

Everything has to happen in the correct order. The reader needs to know when things happen.

1 Decide if your journey will be long or short. A week? A month?

2 Write down the year at the beginning.

3 Use your answers to the questions on page 48 to help you write your journal.

4 Remember to write the date and place every time you begin a new day. You can also write what happens over several days by writing: 'From Monday 4th April to Wednesday 6th April, Indian Ocean.'

5 Your journey can be on a modern ship or an old ship.

6 Write your journal by hand, in your best writing. You could also include drawings. When you finish it, write a title at the beginning.

Model writing

This is the journal of Elisha Broom, daughter of Captain John Broom of the cruise ship *Sea Horizon*

Whales of the Indian Ocean

Monday, 4 April to Wednesday, 6 April 2012, Red Sea to Indian Ocean

It's very hot and I lie in the shade all day. It's cooler on deck early in the morning or in the evening, but the rest of the time it is 40 degrees. I looked for fish and saw some dolphins today. I'm so bored!

Thursday, 7 April, Indian Ocean

My dad tells me that we should see blue whales soon but they travel alone or sometimes in pairs. As the largest mammal in the world they can grow to 24 metres long. Dad said a marine biologist will give a talk on board tonight about the ocean and its life... hope it is not boring!

Friday, 8 April

Not bored now. At dawn we spotted a female blue whale and her calf. They came really close to the ship. I could see them really clearly — it was amazing!

A blue whale and her calf

49

Revise and check

Vocabulary

1 Read these sentences. Write words or phrases that mean the same as the emboldened words.

   a Unless urgent action is taken, these amazing creatures could become **extinct**.

   b In 2000, the drowned cities were discovered as well as the **ancient** harbour.

   c We were travelling now on a **lagoon** when the trail began to tremble.

2 Write a sentence for each phrase.

   a good cause

   b lend a hand

   c a ripple of applause

3 Write down four words that mean the same as:

   a observe

   b replica

   c journal

   d voyage

Punctuation

1 Add a colon, semicolons, and a full stop to this sentence.

   This is the shopping list two large fresh tomatoes one packet of noodles 500 grams of cheese one kilo of oranges a small bag of rice

2 Add two adjectives before each of the two nouns. Also add punctuation.

   a A _____ _____ car   **b** A _____ _____ baby

3 Punctuate this sentence.

   My brother is tall but my father and mother are not.

Grammar

1 **Choose the correct subordinating connectives to complete these sentences.**

which   what   since   where   that   why   who   when

a The house _____ my friend lives has a blue door _____ will be painted tomorrow.

b I haven't seen her _____ last week _____ she fell off the wall after school.

2 **Make up three sentences placing the clause 'when I am hungry' in a different place in each sentence.**

3 **Write out the sentences below. Then write simple, compound or complex after the right one.**

a She ate her meal and then she did her homework.

b John Ramsay says she's aboard for the Gentlemen and officers, so they might have fresh cream when they please.

c He walked to school.

4 **Chose two modals from the list below to add to this complex sentence.**

should will can must

You _____ do your homework, so that you _____ watch your favourite programme later.

5 **Make these adverbs into adjectives.**

carefully   dangerously   quickly   heavily

Spelling

1 **Complete these words with the correct 'shun' ending.**

-cian -sion -ssion -tion -otion -ution -ition -ation

musi _____   discu _____   direc _____   explor _____

instit _____   emo _____   pos _____   sta _____

4 Ancient civilizations

Pyramids and Sphinx at Giza

Hieroglyphs

LETTER	HIEROGLYPH	DEPICTED	MEANING OF HIEROGLYPH
A		Egyptian vulture	strong personality
B		foot	loves to travel
C K X		basket	lucky
D		hand	friendly
		reed leaf	knightly
		viper	purposeful
		jug stand	stabile
	or	courtyard, flax wick	artful
		two strokes	single-eyed
		cobra	intelligent
L		lion	sedate

MEANING OF HIEROGLYPH	DEPICTED	HIEROG
wise	owl	
pure soul	Red Crown, water surface	or
optimist	lasso	
able to create	wicker seat	
—	hillside	
talkative	mouth	
independent	folded cloth, bolt	or
loves to eat	bread	
obstinate	quail chick	or
equitable	two reed leaf	
capricious	bolt	

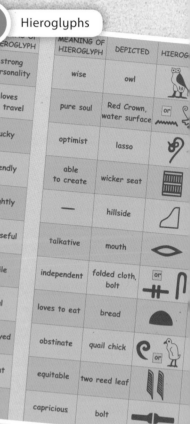

An Egyptian tomb painting

Let's Talk

1 Look at the pictures of items from Ancient Egypt. What do they tell us about the Ancient Egyptians and how they lived?

2 Read the proverb. Talk about what it means. Do you think there is a difference between knowledge and wisdom?

3 Can you think of anything that we use today, which was invented by an ancient civilization?

"Knowledge is not necessarily wisdom."
Proverb from an Ancient Egyptian temple

Ancient Egypt

Learning objective
Prepare, practise, and improve a spoken presentation
or performance.

Word Cloud
carving
chamber
chisel
plaits
temples
tombs

A

Read the paragraphs about the numbered pictures opposite.

1 The pyramids of Giza in Egypt were built from about 2630 BCE. For
a long time, no one was quite sure of their purpose. In fact, they
were built to honour the pharaohs — rulers of Lower Egypt.

2 Ancient Egyptian writing used more than 700 hieroglyphs. Each
hieroglyph was a sign or picture. Many of the pictures were
common objects like a beetle or snake.

3 Ancient Egyptian temples and tombs were painted with scenes
showing Egyptians in traditional dress. Many wore wigs of long
hair, and some of the men had beards, which were usually twisted
into plaits.

B

You have been asked to give a two minute presentation to the
rest of the class on what you know about Ancient Egypt.

▶ You can use four pictures.
Example: a picture of a pyramid at Giza

▶ Make notes for your talk, planning what you will say for each
picture. The first has been done for you.
Example: Explain that this is a pyramid; how they were built
from 2630 BCE to honour the pharaohs.

C

Plan how you will hold your audience's attention.

1 Underline the words you will emphasize.

2 Note where you will give time for the audience to look at
a picture.

3 Practise your talk until you are confident enough to do it in
front of the class.

King Tutankhamun — the most
famous of the pharaohs

Building the pyramid

Learning objective
Consider how characters and settings are presented.

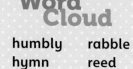

Word Cloud

humbly   rabble
hymn   reed

King Amenemhat has been taken to see how the building of his pyramid is progressing. However, Antef, the bully in charge, has been killed and the workers do not want the King to find out. The person the King thinks is Antef is really a young girl in disguise...

The King's Visit

King Amenemhat was carried in a shaded chair. When he reached the pyramid he opened the curtain and looked out. His face was as calm as the carved lions in the temple, but inside he was excited.

He watched the Boat Gang heaving on the ropes and singing a hymn.
5 A hymn about their glorious King Amenemhat. His Majesty was pleased.

Walking alongside the Boat Gang was a little man with a perfumed wig and a plaited beard. Between the lines of the hymn the King could hear the little man shouting. It was not very pleasant.

"You are the biggest bunch of brainless beetles on this pyramid and all
10 you can do is sing. You can't move one little stone and you think it's something to sing about?" he shouted in his voice that was thin as a Nile reed.

He raised the whip and tried to crack it. The end of the whip lashed back and caught him on the end of his nose.

15 "Don't laugh, you rabble of rats! Ouch! Ouch! Ouch! If one man laughs, I will have him taken to the top of the pyramid and thrown off! Now h-e-a-v-e!"

King Amenemhat said to a servant, "Send Antef to me."

The servant hurried off and brought the little work-driver
20 back. Antef held a hand to his injured nose and kept his eyes on the sizzling sand. All King Amenemhat could see was the dark wig and the plaited beard.

"Is the work going well, Antef?" the King asked. "You shout at them a lot!"

"Ah, but only because we all love you so much, we want to do better than our best for you," Antef said humbly.

"Better than your best. Is that the best you can do?"

"It's better." Antef muttered, "May I get back to work now, Your Majesty? They will be dropping that stone in place soon and I need to be there – we don't want any more accidents."

"Any more?" the King said. "Have there been any others?"

"No, your Majesty," Antef said, a little confused. "Just the odd crushed beetle. Nothing to worry about."...

The King leaned forward and peered at the work-driver. "Are you all right, Antef?"

"Sorry, Your Majesty," he sniffled. "It was my favourite beetle."

From *The Plot on the Pyramid* by Terry Deary

Comprehension

Learning objective
Analyse the success of writing in evoking particular moods, e.g. suspense.

A

Give evidence from the text to support your answers.

1 The extract in line three says of the King, '...but inside he was excited.' Why was the King excited?

2 The extract also says, `His Majesty was pleased.' Why was he pleased?

3 The young girl disguised as Antef does various things to stop her face being seen. Find one example in the extract.

B

What do you think?

1 Find one example of alliteration used by the young girl pretending to be Antef, and then explain why you think she has used it.

2 Why do you think a reader would want to read on? What would they want to find out?

C

What about you?

What do you think Antef should do next?

Glossary

heave to lift or move something heavy

muttered spoken in a low voice

peered looked at something closely or with difficulty

sniffled breathing in through the nose when crying or during a cold

55

Direct speech

Learning objective
Punctuate speech and use apostrophes accurately.

When you use direct speech in your own stories check that the punctuation is correct. Also, remember that for each new speaker the text needs to start on a new line.

Example: The King leaned forward and peered at the work-driver. "Are you all right, Antef?"
"Sorry, Your Majesty," he sniffled. "It was my favourite beetle."

Sometimes, try to use more precise verbs than 'said'.
Examples: sniffled, muttered, shouted

You could even add adverbs.
Examples: loudly, quietly

A

Rewrite the text below, starting new lines for new speakers. Replace 'said' with other verbs. Perhaps add some adverbs too.

'I want to go swimming," said Soo Young. "I can't stand staying indoors all day." "I thought you had homework to do," said Mum. "Oh Mum," said Soo Young. "I've almost finished it. Can't I just take an hour off." "Yes," said Mum. "But only when you've finished your work." "But the pool will be closed if I don't go soon!" said Soo Young. "Then you'd better get going," said Mum.

B

Rewrite the following dialogue, inserting correct punctuation and starting new lines for new speakers.

Excuse me, said the man. Can you tell me what the time is? He gestured towards his wrist. I seem to have left my watch at home. He laughed. I am becoming very forgetful in my old age! I think it's about 8 o'clock, said Imran,w laughing. I actually haven't got my watch on, but I do remember seeing the time on the town hall clock. The town hall! said the man. That's just the place I'm looking for. Can you point me in the right direction? Certainly, Imran said.

Remember: Put punctuation, such as commas, inside the speech marks:
"I'll go now," he said.
NOT
"I'll go now", he said.

C

1 Write a short conversation which involves two speakers, but forget to take a new line when you should, and use 'said' throughout.

2 Give this to a partner to write out correctly.

The origins of words

Learning objective
Explore word origins and the use of words from other languages.

The English language that we use today has many different origins. Words have come from different countries, with many words formed around Greek or Latin roots.

Example: 'hieros' means holy, and 'glyph' means carving, so that's how we get the word 'hieroglyphic.'

A

Find the Latin or Greek root word in each of the words below. Use the table of meanings to help you.

**chilli con carne   sensitive   vitamin   carnivorous
annual   anniversary   vitality   sensible**

Greek or Latin root	Meaning
ann	year
carn	meat
sens	feel, be aware
vit	life

Challenge

Using an etymological dictionary, find out where these words came from: hurricane, cafe, alphabet, algebra, ketchup.

B

The same roots, prefixes and suffixes are used in lots of words. Think of two words to add to this word web using the same prefix tele– and the suffix –ible.

television

tele———

visible

———ible

C

Throughout history, the English language has borrowed many words from other languages through travel, exploration, or even war.

1   Read the words that come from each of these countries in the table below.

2   Find the the six countries on the map.

Urdu/Hindi: pyjamas, shampoo, bungalow

Mexican: chocolate

Greek: theatre, orchestra, chorus

Italian: piano, umbrella

Turkish: coffee, yoghurt

Iranian: sofa, caravan

57

Ancient Egyptian authors

Learning objective
Recognize key characteristics of a non-fiction historical text.

Scribes in Ancient Egypt

How do we know so much about Ancient Egypt?
Unlike some ancient civilizations, Egypt had a writing system. Without these written records, we would know far less about ancient Egypt today. We can read about important historical
5   events, like the lives and deaths of pharaohs. There are also details of everyday life, like legal contracts, tax records, family trees, medical treatments, plans, and lists for building the pyramids, stores of food and work tools.

Who were the scribes?
10   The scribes who compiled these written records were members of a specialist profession and many were the children of scribes. Nearly all were boys. Scribes had a privileged position in society: they did not pay taxes or work in the fields or do military service. In fact, the Egyptian word for 'sesh' or scribe doesn't simply mean
15   someone who reads or writes, but someone who draws and creates.

A scribe's instruments

How long did it take to train a scribe?
Young children started at Scribe School at the age of five. First they had to study how to read and write hieroglyphs. This
20   meant learning more than 700 of these picture symbols by heart. They also studied maths, law, history and geography, and the ablest ones were taught engineering and architecture too.
25   Discipline was strict, and school teachers made their pupils work hard. Lazy boys were beaten, or expelled. In fact, the Egyptian word for 'teach' ('seba') also means 'beat'. It took about 10–12 years
30   for students to complete their studies; then they were ready to go out to work.

What tools and materials did scribes use?

Pictures often show scribes with the tools of their trade: a roll of papyrus writing material, reed pens and brushes and jars of black and red ink. Because papyrus was valuable, student scribes practised writing hieroglyphs on fragments of clay tablets. Both black and red ink were used: red was used for headings and titles, and to correct mistakes – a practice that continues today.

What jobs did qualified scribes do?

Scribes played an important part in the administration of the kingdoms and were highly respected. In addition, people couldn't read or write so a large percentage of the population used scribes to write letters for them, and also to read aloud any letters that they received.

Glossary

administration controlling or managing something

discipline teaching people to control themselves and follow rules

expelled sent away from a school

family trees diagrams that show all the people in a family

privileged having something special that only a few people have

tax records details of money that has been paid to the government

tools of their trade work tools needed for their particular job

Comprehension

A

Explain your answers using words and phrases from the text.

1   Give two reasons why writing was important to Egyptian society.

2   Find one piece of evidence in the extract that shows that scribes were highly valued.

3   In three to four sentences, describe a typical day at Scribe School. Begin like this:

    An important part of the day's lesson was...

B

What do you think?

To help readers follow a non-fiction text, writers often:

▶ use subheadings so that the reader knows what each paragraph is about

▶ make a big, general point, then give examples

▶ explain new vocabulary.

Do you think the extract writer has used these methods well? Find an example of each.

C

What about you?

Which three facts in the passage did you find the most interesting, and why?

Challenge

What is papyrus made from? Research the answer on the Internet.

Discussion time

All the children at Scribe School had to study maths, law, history, and geography, as well as writing.

Which of these subject do you think are the most important to learn today, and why?

Word classes

> **Learning objective**
> Revise different word classes.

The verb is the most important word in a sentence. It tells us what happens. Verbs are either finite or non-finite. Finite verbs have subjects, non-finite forms do not. Using non-finite forms can give your writing added interest.

One non-finite form is the **infinitive**. It is usually two words, but is sometimes contracted to one.

Example: Mary longed **to go** abroad. I helped her **(to) pack**.

A

Make up sentences using each of the following infinitive verbs.

to sneeze   to jump   to go   to hit   to run   to sit

Another non-finite verb form is the **present participle** – that is, verbs which end in **–ing**.

Example: He stormed out of the room, **slamming** the door behind him.
Walking up the garden path, he noticed how everything was in bloom.

B

1   Use the following present participle verbs in the **middle** of a sentence.

running   shouting   hitting   sobbing   smashing   stumbling

2   Use the same present participle verbs at the **beginning** of a sentence.

C

Here is a table with some past participle verbs

Verb	Past participle
To beat	beaten
To eat	eaten
To fall	fallen
To give	given

Use each of the past participle verbs above in a sentence.

Try writing some sentences that start with a present participle.

Active and passive

Learning objective
Explore the use of active and passive verbs within a sentence.

When the verb is **active** in a sentence, it is the subject performing the action, and the object of the sentence is the receiver of that action.

Example: The mouse frightened the elephant.

When the verb is **passive**, the sentence is turned around so that the object becomes the subject.

Example: The elephant was frightened by the mouse.

A

Change these sentences in the active voice to the passive. The first one has been done for you.

The queen ate the jam tarts. → The jam tarts were eaten by the queen.

1 Mrs Smith has made a cake.
2 The birds had eaten all the plants.
3 Everybody here loathes cruelty to animals.
4 We all enjoyed the 'Superman' film.
5 The children cooked dinner.

B

Change the passive voice into the active in these sentences.
1 Her answer was given in a low voice.
2 The strike has been called off by the workmen.
3 All his pocket money has been spent.
4 The telephone was answered by the maid.
5 The lock had been forced by an intruder.

C

Which sentence in each pair has its verb in the active voice?
1 The dog had bitten the cat again.
   The cat has been bitten again by the dog.
2 Smoked fish is not liked by everyone.
   Not everyone likes smoked fish.
3 The grass should be cut this weekend.
   I should cut the grass this weekend.

Kennings

Learning objective
Explore how poets manipulate and play with words and their sounds.

Word Cloud
hunter
keeper
teller
villain

This poem is a kenning. The lines are made up of two words joined together with a hyphen, making a new word. The *Historian* poem uses these new words to describe the different ways of being a *historian* (someone who studies the past).

Historian

Time-detective
Bone-collector
Stone-saver
Rune-reader
5 Parchment-keeper
Villain-hounder
Hero-maker
Grave-digger
Fact-hunter
10 Story-searcher
Truth-seeker
Year-counter
Age-teller
Past-banker

John Kitching

An archaeologists at a dig

Who is this?

Stripey-starer
Eyeline-wearer
Hook-holder
Snake-bearer
5 Beard-plaiter
Necklace-prisoner
Gold-giver
Gold-taker

Eleanor Watts

CLUE: THERE IS A PICTURE OF HIM IN THIS UNIT.

Comprehension

A

Poet's use of language

1 In the poem *Historian*, find joined-up words that could mean:

   a a historian who likes a person from history

   b a historian who dislikes a person from history

2 Explain why the poet calls a historian:

   a time-detective   **b** rune-reader

3 Kennings often use alliteration, as in **s**tone-**s**aver. Find one more example of alliteration in *Historian*.

Glossary

hounder hunter

parchment an old-fashioned writing paper, sometimes made from goat-skin

rune a letter of the alphabet used in the past by people in northern Europe

B

What do you think?

1 Who do you think the poem *Who is this?* on page 62 is about? If you can't guess, look at the pictures on page 53. Do you know now? How?

2 Why do you think the king is called a 'necklace-prisoner'?

3 Who do you think the king gives gold to and takes gold from?

4 Who is the person in the poem below? How do you know?

C

What about you?

1 Make up your own kenning about a present occupation, such as a teacher, doctor or nurse. Use new joined-up words and try to use alliteration.

2 Read your kenning aloud. Ask your class to guess who your kenning describes.

Who is this?

Nightmare-wiper

Morning-waker

Sock-finder

Lunchbox-maker

5 Hair-comber

Quarrel-queller

School-runner

Story-teller

Problem-solver

10 Love-giver

Wise-worrier

Life-giver

Eleanor Watts

Narrative story structure

Learning objective
Understand aspects of narrative structure.

All stories have a similar structure.

▶ The **setting** tells us when and where it happened.

▶ The **characters** are the people in the story.

▶ The **problem** makes us want to read on to find out what happened.

▶ The **climax** is the most exciting point when something terrible or wonderful could happen.

▶ The **resolution** is how the problem is fixed and explains how the story ends.

Model writing

Read the story on pages 54–55 again. Next, answer the questions to help you see the structure of the story.

Setting and characters

1 Where is the story set?

2 Who are the main characters?

Problem

3 Why don't the men want the King to know what happened to Antef?

4 How does the young girl disguise herself as Antef, the work-driver?

5 Why does she look down as the King speaks to her?

Climax

6 The girl makes a mistake when she speaks to the King. What does she say?

Resolution

7 How does the girl resolve the problem?

8 There is a bigger problem to resolve. What do you think happens in the end?

Writing a narrative story

Learning objective
Plan plot, characters, and structure effectively in writing a narrative story.

Write an escape story

Write a short story called *Escape*. This should be five or six paragraphs long.

1 Plan your story first.

Setting	Grab the reader's attention with an exciting opening. Tell the reader where and when it happens. Use powerful adjectives and verbs to set the atmosphere.
Characters	Describe no more than two characters. What do they look like? How do they speak?
Problem	Why are they in danger? Who or what is threatening them? Use some short sentences for suspense.
Climax	What must they escape from? Use similes or metaphors to help the reader imagine the danger.
Resolution	How do they get away? Does the story end happily for everyone?

Top Tip

Each episode could end with a 'cliff-hanger', which makes the reader want to find out what happens next.

2 Plan the vocabulary you will use. Try to use strong verbs to keep the plot moving and use powerful adjectives.

3 Write your story then check and edit it using the table above.

5 Spies and mystery

Alex Rider, a teenage spy and hero of many adventures, such as in the film, *Stormbreaker*

The *Spy Kids* movies are popular all over the world.

"Life is a struggle and a good spy goes in there and fights."
Harriet the Spy

Let's Talk

1 A spy wears a disguise so they are not recognized. If you were a spy, what would you change about how you look, move and speak so that no one knew it was you?

2 What genre do you think the Alex Rider spy books belong to?

Spy words uncovered

Many spy stories from books have been made into films like *Alex Rider: Stormbreaker*

Learning objective

Explore definitions and use new words in context.

A

Here are some new words found in spy books and films. Match the words with the correct definition.

Example: Spymaster = 7

bug   code   intelligence   secret agent

spymaster   surveillance   alias

Definitions

1 Useful information
2 A hidden microphone which records conversation
3 Watching someone over a period of time
4 Another term for a spy
5 A false name and identity
6 Letters and numbers used to send hidden messages
7 A person who controls several spies

B

Fill in the blanks with some of the words and phrases above.

I am a _____ and my a _____ is _____ [you decide what your 'spy name' is]. I like to hide an electronic _____ to record what people are saying. When I need to send a message I use _____ . I pretend that I am a travel agent which means that I can carry out _____ and nobody is suspicious.

C

Crack the code by working out the code letters and rewrite the sentence.

Dxngzr! Thzrz xrz rumyurs yf x dyublz xgznt.

Mystery and suspense

Learning objective
Comment on the writer's use of language, demonstrating awareness of its impact on the reader.

Word Cloud

agent   preposterous
assignment   resourceful
blackmailing   snoop
enterprise

Alex Rider's uncle was mysteriously killed. Alex discovers he was a spy and is asked to continue his uncle's mission to stop the villain, Herod Sayle at Sayle Enterprises, giving free but dangerous 'Stormbreaker' computers to all schools. But Alex doesn't want to be a spy…

Alex becomes a spy

"Who are you?" Alex asked. "What do you want with me?"

"My name is Blunt, I am Chief Executive of the Special Operations Division of MI6. Mrs Jones here is our Head of Special Operations. She gave your uncle his last assignment," he replied…

5   "What we're suggesting is that you come and work for us," Mrs Jones said. "We have enough time to give you some basic training – not that you'll need it, probably. You'll be able to meet Herod Sayle, keep an eye on him, and tell us what you think. Perhaps you'll also find out what it was that your uncle discovered and why he had to die. You shouldn't be

10 in any danger. After all, who would suspect a fourteen-year-old boy of being a spy?"

"All we're asking you to do is to report back to us," Blunt said. "That's all we want. Two weeks of your time. A chance to make sure these computers are everything they're cracked up to be. A chance to

15 serve your country."

"No," Alex said.

"I'm sorry?"

"It's a dumb idea. I don't want to be a spy. I want to be a footballer. Anyway, I have a life of my own!" He found it

20 difficult to choose the right words. The whole thing was so preposterous he almost wanted to laugh. "Why don't you ask this Felix Lester to snoop around for you?"

"We don't believe he'd be as resourceful as you,"

25 Blunt said.

"He's probably better at computer games." Alex shook his head. "I'm sorry. I'm just not interested. I don't want to get involved."

"That's a pity," Blunt said. "Then we'd better move on to discuss your future," he continued. "Ian Rider has of course left the house and all his money to you. However, he left it in trust until you are twenty-one. And we control that trust. You'll be sent to an institution."

"You're blackmailing me!" Alex exclaimed.

"Not at all."

"But if I agree to do what you ask… ?"

Blunt glanced at Mrs Jones. "Help us and we'll help you," she said.

From *Stormbreaker* by Anthony Horowitz

Comprehension

A

Use words and phrases from both the extract and graphic novel page to explain your answers.

1 What do Blunt and Mrs Jones want Alex to do?

2 Look at lines 15 to 20. Which personal pronoun is repeated in these sentences, and why?

3 Blunt uses different methods to persuade Alex to become a spy. Find evidence from the text to match the three methods below.

  a Blunt appeals to his loyalty to his country.

  b Blunt flatters Alex.

  c Blunt blackmails him.

B

Writer's use of language

1 Find **three** differences between the language in the text extract and the language in the graphic novel on this page.

2 What effect does the graphic novel language have on the reader?

C

What about you?

1 Divide the story extract into six boxes to turn it into a graphic novel. Use the line numbers to help you work out how the extract should be divided. You will be telling the same story– but this time through drawing and using speech bubbles for dialogue.

This page from the graphic novel of *Stormbreaker* is also about Alex becoming a spy.

69

Word classes

> ### Learning objective
> Revise different word classes.

A

Read the extract from *Stormbreaker* on pages 68–69.

1 From the extract, find **three** examples of each word class and complete the table. The first one is an example to help you.

Word class	Example	Three more examples from the extract
Common noun	boy	**time, uncle, danger**
Proper noun	Mrs Jones	
Verb (including a verb phrase)	are suggesting	
Adjective	enough time	
Personal pronoun	you	
Preposition	to	

2 From the *Stormbreaker* extract, find one example of each of these word classes:

- ❯ adverb
- ❯ coordinating conjunction
- ❯ subordinating connective

B

Write ten sentences on what you did last weekend. When you have finished, underline examples of the following: common nouns, proper nouns, adjectives, verbs/verb phrases, adverbs, personal pronouns, prepositions, coordinating conjunctions and subordinating connectives.

> ### Challenge
> Start some of your sentences from Exercise C with an adverb and a subordinating connective.

C

Rewrite the ten sentences so that you have more:

- ❯ adjectives
- ❯ adverbs

I GET *GADGETS?*

Relative clauses

> **Learning objective**
> Distinguish the main clauses and other clauses in a complex sentence.

A relative clause tells us which particular person or thing the writer means. We use **who** when we are talking about people.

Example: A school teacher is someone who teaches students.

A

Insert who, which or that into these sentences.

1 What is the best book_____you have ever read?

2 The students_____we met last night were very funny.

3 The girl___I wanted to see was not there.

4 The coat____Marcia borrowed has been lost.

5 What happened to the purse____was on the chair?

B

From each of these two sentences make one sentence with a relative clause. Use *who, that,* or *which*. You will need to start the new sentence with 'The'.

1 A spy was injured in the helicopter crash. He is now in hospital.

2 A train goes to the airport. It leaves once every hour.

3 An apartment was completely submerged by the flood. It is no longer there.

4 A secret agent complained to her boss. She was very rude.

C

Correct these sentences.

1 I don't like horror films who are too frightening.

2 The student which didn't like studying was disappointed with his grades.

3 The accident what happened was all my fault.

4 The book is about a spy girl which goes on amazing adventures.

Learning objective
Analyse how paragraphs and chapters are structured and linked.

Word Cloud

compass   ingenious
constructing   sprinkled
devices

Spy gadgets

All spies use clever devices called gadgets. In the
James Bond movies the character 'Q' designs all
the spy gadgets. He is based on a real man,
Charles Fraser-Smith, who created some of the
5 most amazing gadgets during World War II.

The past

During the war, Fraser-Smith thought up
ingenious solutions to difficult problems. As a
small compass sewn into clothes could be
10 detected, he decided to put magnetized
needles inside matchsticks. The match could
be dropped in a pool of water and
point north, acting exactly like a compass.

The future

15 Gadgets and devices have become more
important in spying. How we spy will change in the future
as human agents can be easily seen and caught, but machines and gadgets
can be made to destroy themselves if discovered. It also helps that gadgets
are very tiny. Nanotechnology is the science of constructing microscopic
20 machines, called 'nanobots' (tiny robots). These could be sprinkled like dust
over electronic equipment and into rooms to send back information.

A submarine disguised as a crocodile

When wet, the top layer of these playing
cards can be peeled back to show a map.

Glossary

magnetized turned into a
magnet (a piece of metal that
attracts iron and steel
towards it)

microscopic not visible with
the human eye; only seen
through a microscope

Comprehension

A

Give evidence from the extract to support your answers to A and B.

1 What is the purpose of the first paragraph?

2 Why has the author divided up the text this way?

3 What else on these two pages gives us information?

B

What do you think?

1 Which gadget do you think is the most useful?

2 In what way do you think gadgets will be very different in the future?

C

What about you?

1 Imagine you have been asked to explain to a younger student what spying is. Write down what you would say to them.

2 Invent a new gadget for a spy. Prepare a speech and presentation to explain it to the class.

Discussion time
Discuss whether there is such a thing as 'good' spying and 'bad' spying. Can you explain the difference?

A future nanobot, shaped like a crab, scuttles across an electronic circuit board.

This dragonfly micro aerial vehicle (MAV) is tiny and weighs less than a quarter of a gram. Future MAVs may be able to hover or fly unnoticed, spying on people or photographing documents.

Making writing clear

Learning objective
Understand and use dashes and brackets.

Writers use punctuation to separate words, phrases or clauses to make the meaning clearer for the reader.

Examples:

Commas: Juni Cortez, a secret agent, wears high-tech glasses.

Dashes: Juni Cortez — a secret agent — wears high-tech glasses.

Brackets: Juni Cortez (a secret agent) wears high-tech glasses.

Commas separate the phrase or clause from the rest of the sentence, dashes emphasise it and brackets decrease its importance. Brackets give extra information without breaking the flow of the sentence.

A

Write the sentences below twice. First, use dashes to separate the underlined phrase. Second, use brackets to separate it.

1 Alex took a coin <u>all he had in his pocket</u> and passed it to his friend.

2 Complete the form in ink <u>not pencil</u> and give it to the teacher.

3 The spy moved <u>very suddenly</u> towards me.

B

Place the extra information given in brackets at a suitable point in the sentence.

1 Charles Dickens is a famous writer.   **(1812–1870)**

2 For this recipe you need 2 kilograms of flour.   **(Finest)**

3 I need to borrow five hundred dollars from the bank.   **($500)**

4 She finally answered that she didn't understand the question.
                    (after taking five minutes to think about it)

- Use commas to separate information in a straightforward way.

- Use dashes to separate and emphasize information.

- Use brackets to separate information in a hidden way>

Speech marks

Learning objective
Punctuate speech correctly.

The extract from *Stormbreaker* makes clear how direct speech should be laid out and punctuated.

"No," Alex said.

"I'm sorry?"

"It's a dumb idea. I don't want to be a spy. I want to be a footballer. Anyway, I have a life of my own!" He found it difficult to choose the right words… "Why don't you ask this Felix Lester to snoop around for you?"

"We don't believe he'd be as resourceful as you," Blunt said.

A

Using this extract as your model, write out the rules for:

▶ using speech marks when someone is speaking
▶ where commas should be placed when speech marks are used
▶ when someone speaking asks a question
▶ when someone speaking makes an exclamation
▶ what to do when someone new speaks
▶ what to do when the speech is 'interrupted' by a reporting clause.

B

Correct the errors in the written conversation below and set out the dialogue properly.

Are you coming out tonight? Alexa asked. No, I can't replied Sabrina. I have spy training. Do you want to come and watch the training session? No thanks, Alexa replied, feeling really disappointed. She had wanted Sabrina to come out with her tonight. It was her birthday after all. Alexa folded her arms and looked at her friend sadly. Oh, come on Alexa, don't be cross replied Sabrina. Let's go out afterwards. How about it?

Spy poem

Learning objective
Explore how the poet manipulates and plays with words and their sounds.

Word Cloud

elementary   uncovering
locate   unrivalled
stealthy

My Dad's a Secret Agent

My dad's a secret agent.

He's an undercover spy.

He's the world's best detective.

4 He's the perfect private eye.

He's a Pinkerton, a gumshoe,

He's a snoop and he's a sleuth.

He's unrivalled at detecting

8 and uncovering the truth.

He's got eyesight like an eagle.

He's got hearing like a bat.

He can out-smell any bloodhound.

12 He's as stealthy as a cat.

He can locate nearly anything

with elementary ease.

But no matter how he looks and looks

16 my dad can't find his keys!

Kenn Nesbitt

The Pinkerton National Detective Agency was founded in the USA in 1850. This is the original logo.

Comprehension

A

Give evidence from the poem to support your answers.

1 Find three other words in the poem that mean the same as 'spy'.

2 Find three examples when you think the poet is exaggerating the abilities of his dad.

3 Why has the poet decided to leave the fact that his dad cannot find his keys until the last line?

B

Poet's use of language

1 The poet has not used two of the techniques below, which ones are they?

   a alliteration   b simile   c lines of different lengths
   d every line rhymes   e words repeated

2 Find an example in the poem to illustrate two of the techniques the poet did use.

3 Why has the poet used an exclamation mark at the end?

Poetry performance

Learning objective

Prepare, practise, and improve a spoken performance.

Glossary

bloodhound a dog who uses his nose to follow a scent

gumshoe slang word meaning 'investigator'

sleuth another term for a detective

A

In groups read the poem on page 76 together.

1 Practise reading it aloud together in rhythm.

2 Now, each person read a line aloud in turn.

3 All together, read the first verse aloud quietly, then get louder towards the end of the poem.

B

Prepare and practise in your group.

1 As a group write an extra verse. This could still be about the keys. Remember to include: 4 lines; lines of the same length; alternate lines that rhyme; simile or alliteration, and a funny last line. Read the whole poem aloud to the class.

C

As a class listen to all the groups present their reading of the poem. Discuss the new verses written by the groups and give them feedback about their choice of language and their presentation of the poem.

Heroes and villains

You are the hero/heroine

Write a description of yourself as the hero or heroine. You are going to be quite ordinary in comparison to the villain. You will need to write about yourself in the third person.

Example:

Name:	Description:
	He/she has a large mop of untidy hair and a small, inquisitive nose. The hair looked as if it hadn't been combed in a long, long time. It reminded people who saw him/her of an old bird's nest.

Story starters

Getting started

Now you have a hero or heroine, let's begin the story.

Stormbreaker begins like this:

"When the doorbell rings at three in the morning it is never good news."

Here are four examples of story openings. Choose the one you like best.

1 She could see the curtains move in the moonlight. Was that something moving outside?

2 He heard the soft squeal of a car's tyres behind him and walked faster. The car went faster too...

3 Good evening, sir, we are arresting you on suspicion of...

4 Lucy got into the car without thinking. It was kind of them to send a car to collect her. She turned to thank the driver when suddenly she realized who he was...

Now write your one beginning to a suspense story. You've got a villain and yourself as the secret hero or heroine. You should end your writing at the most exciting bit, with readers wondering, 'What is going to happen next?

Top Tips

▶ Use rich verbs like snarl, growl, whisper, shout, bellow.

▶ Let your characters speak. Pretend in your head that you're talking: 'Look out! He's behind you!'

▶ Use some great adjectives: 'He looked like a wrinkled toad.'

▶ Make your story move by using words such as: later, after some time, soon.

6 Extreme Earth

Volcanic lava cooled and hardened

Satellite picture of a tornado

Let's Talk

Look at the examples of Extreme Earth in the pictures.

1 What has happened in the volcanic photo?

2 What is about to happen to the town in the large photo?

3 What extreme weather or events have happened in your country? Explain them to a partner.

> "Should you shield the canyons from the windstorms you would never see the true beauty of their carvings."
>
> Elizabeth Kubler-Ross

Extreme events

🌍 **Learning objective**

Express and explain ideas clearly.

Explore definitions and use new words in context.

Word Cloud

arctic   flood
avalanche   hurricane
desert   lava
drought   tornado
earthquake   tsunami
eruption   volcano

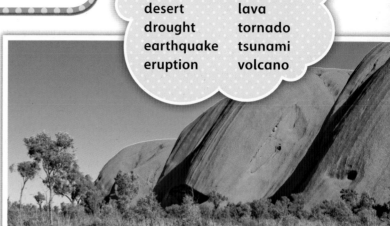

A

1 Match the pictures to the right caption.

  a desert   **b** tornado   **c** volcano

2 Which of the Word Cloud words describe extreme environments and which describe extreme weather events?

3 Choose two terms from the Word Cloud and explain them to a partner in your own words using:

  ▶ only 30 words   ▶ clear, precise language

Example: Earthquakes are the result of the shaking, rolling, and sudden shocks that occur in the Earth's surface.

B

This explanation of how a volcano erupts has been mixed up. Put the sentences in the right order 1–5.

a The Earth's crust is made up of huge slabs called plates, which fit together like a jigsaw puzzle. These plates sometimes move.

b Below the Earth's crust is a substance called magma, which is made of rocks and gases.

c When the plates collide, magma is squeezed up between the plates.

d When magma erupts through the Earth's surface it is called lava.

e Volcanoes are like giant safety valves that release the pressure that builds up inside the Earth.

Volcano story

Learning objective
Consider the writer's use of language and how characters and settings are presented.

This story is set over a thousand years ago in the town of Herculaneum in Italy, just as the volcano, Vesuvius, erupts. Petronia, the main character, is a servant girl and Lavinia is her mistress.

Mount Vesuvius erupts

At that moment, the ground seemed to heave below her feet. Then the most deafening sound Petronia had ever heard shook the house. It seemed to come from the very bowels of the earth.

From the kitchen she could hear screams and the sound of shattering dishes. The mistress rushed into the dining room followed by two maids who had been doing her hair. She was
5 wearing only her sleeveless undertunic. Strands of hair hung down from a half-secured bun, and a streak of red hair dye trickled down her cheek. Her eyes were wide with fear.

"In Juno's name, what is it? What is happening?" she cried.

The master emerged from the garden, his face a mask.

"We must go back to Rome," he announced. "I should have listened to the others at the
10 baths. Many of them have left already. Gather everyone together. We will leave immediately. Slave, bring the horses!" he called, striding out of the room.

Lavinia's face was white and pinched.

"Petronia, fetch all the valuables," she ordered. "Put everything here, on the table. The silver and gold, the statues of Isis, everything you can carry. Cook, find some bags, Lena, get the baby,
15 and... my jewel case. It's in my bedroom. Quickly!" she screamed.

Petronia began running around the house with the others, plucking statues from their stands, bronze lamps and dishes from the side table — anything valuable that wasn't too heavy to carry. Everything was brought to the dining room, where the mistress shoved as much as she could into large coarse sacks.

20 A second cracking sound shook the house, not as loud as the first, but longer. A strange stench filled the air, like rotten eggs. For the first time, Petronia noticed that the bright sunshine had disappeared, and the sky had turned an odd shade — not gray like storm clouds, or black like night, but dirty brown, like...

Like death, she thought.

From *The Secrets of Vesuvius* by Sara Bisel

This painting of Vesuvius was made in 1776 by Joseph Wright

Comprehension

A

Give evidence from the extract to support your answers.

1 Find two phrases or sentences in the extract that show the volcano was erupting. *Example:* 'The ground seemed to heave below her feet.'

2 Which two sentences sum up the action the master wants to take to escape the volcano?

    a "We must go back to Rome."

    b "I should have listened to the others at the baths."

    c "Many of them have left already."

    d "Gather everyone together."

    e "We will leave immediately."

3 Petronia grabbed some items for her mistress. Which two reasons explain what she decided to take?

    a They were light.

    b They were large.

    c They were in the dining room.

    d They were valuable.

4 What evidence from the text suggests that the family might not make it to Rome?

B

Writer's presentation of character

1 Why did Lavinia's face look white and pinched?

2 Although the master is afraid of what might happen, he still stays very much in control over how he speaks, what he says, who he gives orders to and how he moves. Find evidence of this in the extract.

The first one has been done for you.

How he speaks	'He announced.'
What he says	
Who he gives orders to	
How he moves	

C

What about you?

Imagine you have to report the event for television news. You need to decide on:

▶ The headline

▶ Three or four main facts/events

▶ Interview comments from the master, Lavina and Petronia

▶ How to end the report

Glossary

bowels of the earth deep under the ground

bun hair fastened in a small round shape at the back of someone's head

coarse if a material is coarse, it has a rough surface or texture

emerged came out from a place

plucking removing something by pulling it quickly

trickle to move slowly like a thin stream of water

Different language for different texts

Learning objective
Revise language conventions and grammatical features of different types of texts.

Depending on the type of text, writers use language, grammar and punctuation in different ways. For example, a formal report doesn't use questions or exclamation marks, but a story does. This is because they help show the characters' feelings.

Example: "It's in my bedroom. Quickly!" she screamed.
"In Juno's name, what is it? What is happening?" she cried.

A

In this extract the characters are experiencing extreme emotions. Replace the punctuation with new question marks, exclamation marks and ellipses to help convey the emotions.

'Oh no, what's happening,' cried Ahmed. 'Why are all those rocks falling from the mountain. Oh no. It's a landslide. We're trapped. We're trapped. We can't get out.'

'Keep calm,' Fatima ordered.

B

Writers add actions and details about how characters speak.
Examples:

Ahmed lifted his head slowly, and sighed. 'Which way do you think we should go?' he asked, his voice thick with weariness and exhaustion. Gripping his hand even tighter, she shouted, 'I know I'm right ! Let's go!'

C

Add movement, gestures and details of how the characters are speaking to this dialogue.

'I'm frightened! I don't want to go.'

'If we don't go, we'll never get out of here.'

'I don't care. I don't want to go!'

'Come on. Follow me.'

Same sounds but different spelling

Learning objective
Confirm correct choices when representing consonants ck / k / ke / que.

Challenge

Keep a list of words that end in a 'k' sound. Sort them into different spelling columns to help you remember them.

Some sounds seem the same, but different letters can be used to make the same sound. For example, the letters **'ck'**, **'k'**, **'ke'** and **'que'** at the ends of words **all** make a **'k'** sound.

A

Here are some words from the extract, 'Mount Vesuvius Erupts', which end in a 'k' sound. Sort them into different groups based on the spelling at the end of each word.

crack earthquake streak quick take mask shook pluck
black shook sack

B

Here are more words that end in a 'k' sound. Add them to the lists you created in A. You will have to create one more column.

shake sick unique walk smirk antique stick thank lack
junk hook track sleek stark shriek beak stroke quake
rock spike block trunk tweak park wreck

At the end of a word, the letters **'l'**, **'r'**, **'n'** and **'c'** are generally followed by **'k'**. Some of these words can be found in A and B above.

How to choose '–**ick**' or '–**ic**' at the end of words:
Words with one syllable generally end in –**ick**.
Example: 'trick'
Words with more than one syllable generally end in –**ic**.
Example: 'electric'

C

Correct the incorrect spellings below. There are six errors.

As he walked out of the health clinike, the old gentleman suffered a moment of panick at the terrificke amount of traffick passing in front of him. 'No,' he thought. 'I mustn't get too dramatique about it. Nothing horrifik is going to happen.' Boldly, he stepped off the pavement...

The Galápagos Islands

Learning objective
Distinguish between fact and opinion in a recount.

Word Cloud
aerodynamic   species
breeding   unique
conservation

Expedition of a lifetime

I couldn't believe my ears when I got the phone call to say that I was on my way to the Galápagos Islands! I won the trip by entering a photo competition in a wildlife magazine. And
5 now I was about to get the opportunity to do it all again.

    Three months later we were descending over the Galápagos Islands towards Baltra Seymour Airport. What a beautiful sight! The islands lie
10 about 1,000 kilometres off the coast of Ecuador, in the Eastern Pacific Ocean. There are about 13 large islands and six smaller ones, with a population of approximately 25,000. The islands are exceptional in the world. Because of their
15 isolation, unique species developed without any human interference over thousands of years.

Protected species

Our first stop was the Charles Darwin Research Station to see the giant tortoises and to hear
20 about the island's conservation programmes. The tortoises live a leisurely life, and so would you if you weighed 250 kilograms. They eat leaves, grass and cactus, and sleep for up to 16 hours a day. They commonly live to over a hundred
25 years, and the record is 152 years. When Darwin visited in 1835, there were 15 species of tortoise, but now there are only 11 left.

Vegetarian monsters

In the afternoon, we walked down to the beach
30 in search of marine iguanas. Here's a photo of one that I took. It looks incredibly fierce and prehistoric but in fact they are harmless and live off seaweed. When they come onto dry land,

they line up with their heads facing into the wind
35 and sneeze to get rid of the salt that they have taken in.

A mate for life

On our last day, we visited a protected breeding site for the waved albatross on the island of
40 Española. Our ranger told us some fascinating facts about the only tropical albatross in the world. They have a huge wingspan of over two metres and mate for life. The scruffy, downy chicks – we saw some, through binoculars – grow
45 into sleek, aerodynamic adults. When they leave the nest, they spend the next six years at sea off the coast of Peru, returning eventually to the islands to breed.

A life-changing experience

50 We left after an amazing ten days on the islands. Not only was it the most amazing expedition of my life, but it got me interested in conservation programmes, so I think that from now on my life will take a different course.

Comprehension

Learning objective
Distinguish between narrative, fact and opinion in a recount.

Glossary

aerodynamic designed to move well through the air

downy covered in very soft feathers

interference unwanted change or damage

leisurely without hurry

prehistoric from the time in history before events were written down

scruffy untidy and dirty

sleek smooth and shiny

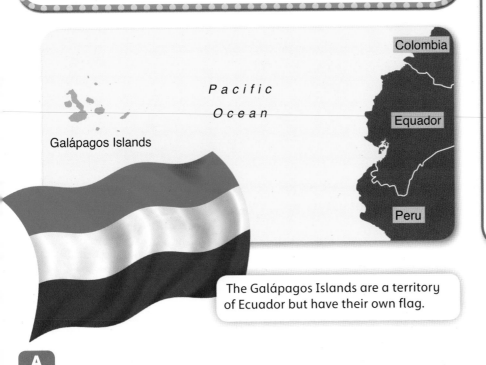

Pacific Ocean

Colombia

Equador

Peru

Galápagos Islands

The Galápagos Islands are a territory of Ecuador but have their own flag.

A

Explain your answers using words and phrases from the extract.

1 What did the author do to win a trip to the Galápagos Islands?

2 Find three facts in the extract.

3 Find three opinions in the extract.

B

What do you think?

1 How did the author feel when he received the phone call?

2 How did the author feel about the idea of visiting the Galápagos Islands?

3 What were the author's impressions of the following: the giant tortoise, the marine iguana, the waved albatross?

C

What about you?

Which places have you visited within/outside your own country to see wildlife?

Discussion time
Your local community has asked students in the area to recommend an animal in the locality that the community can help to protect. Which animal would you chose and why?

Making new words with prefixes and suffixes

Learning objective
Know how to transform meaning with prefixes and suffixes.

A prefix is a group of letters added to the beginning of a word to change the meaning. *Example*: 'pre–' means 'before'. So 'pre–' + 'historic' means 'before history'.

A

Some of the words in the non-fiction extract about the Galápagos Islands contain prefixes. Find words in the extract that use these prefixes.

Prefix	Meaning
con–	with, together
bi–	two, double
inter–	between, involving two or more

Challenge
What do the prefixes 'circum–' and 'contra–' mean?
Find words that begin with these prefixes.

A suffix is a group of letters added to the end of a word to change the meaning. *Example*: '–less' means 'without'. So 'wire' + '–less' means 'without wires'.

B

Which six of the words below can have –less added to the end of them? Use a dictionary to help you.

hope   breed   fact   sleep   harm
home   life   fierce   pain

C

List three words that end with each of these suffixes.

- -able/-ible – able or fit to do something
- -er/-or – someone who does something
- -less – without
- -logy – study of
- -ness – quality/state

Marine biology is the study of underwater life.

Spellings and descriptions

Learning objectives
Further investigate spelling rules and exceptions, including representing unstressed vowels.
Explore definitions and shades of meaning and use new words in context.

Sometimes words have unstressed vowels in them. These are vowels (a, e, i, o, u) that are not easy to hear in words. As a result, they are often missed out in spellings.

A

All these words have unstressed vowels.

**bus_i_ness off_e_ring famil_i_ar diff_e_rent eas_i_ly fam_i_ly
Wedn_e_sday int_e_rest fright_e_ning sep_a_rate gen_e_rous
marv_e_llous mis_e_rable gen_e_rally**

1 Say the words aloud several times, stressing the underlined vowel.

2 Write the words with the underlined vowels enlarged or highlighted. This will help you to remember the vowel.

3 Write sentences using each of these words, spelling them correctly.

B

To describe extreme settings, it is important to pick adjectives carefully and to think about their meanings. Read the description of the inside of a dirty house. Choose one adjective from each pair.

No one had lived in the farmhouse for years. There was a pile of (1) dusty/filthy clothes on the floor in the corner of the kitchen, and a pair of (2) muddy/untidy boots still stood next to the back door that led out into the farmyard. The kitchen was the (3) untidiest/muddiest room I'd ever seen. How had the farmer managed to find things? Magazines were piled in heaps on the table, with packets of cereal and a box of hand tools. Books lay on (4) dusty/filthy shelves and the floor was a (5) grimy/dirty brown colour. A little light came through the (6) grimy/muddy windows, which were covered on the outside with climbing plants.

C

Describe a dirty, neglected place that you know. It could be an old house or apartment building, or a garden. Use words and phrases from B.

Weather poems

Learning objective
Read and interpret poems in which meanings are implied or multi-layered.

Flood

The rain fell all night, beating on roofs
2 as dark and hunched as hills,
cascading uncontained into the street
4 in wind-curved waterfalls.

All night the rain fell, kept falling.
6 This morning, the street's a river:
cars founder and sink, while buses
8 crawl laden as ocean liners,

raise bow-waves so swollen they break
10 booming across the pavement
where tossed at the tide's rising mark
12 seaweed tangles to litter;

and under the hedges and gates
14 fish shoal in the gleaming shallows,
and further out, through the channel
16 marked by wave-slapped traffic-lights,

dolphins leap lampposts, and whales
18 surge and sound in the deep roads.

Dave Calder

Comprehension

A

Use words and phrases from the poem to support your answers.

1 Which statement is true?

   a The poem is about life under the sea.

   b The poem describes the land after there has been a flood.

   c The poem gives a warning about the damage caused by the sea.

2 Find two quotations which show what the poet thinks has happened to vehicles.

B

Poet's use of language

1 The poem has lots of verbs in their **–ing** present participle and **–ed** past participle forms. Make a list of these.

   Example: **–ing** beating, **–ed** hunched

2 In this poem, sea and land become mixed up in the flood: 'bow-waves ... break ... across the pavement'. List the **land-words** and **sea-words** in verses 3–5.

   Example: **Land-words**: pavement, litter
                Sea-words: bow-waves, tide's, seaweed

C

What about you?

What did you like about the poem and what did you find hard to understand? Use examples to answer.

Shape poems

Learning objective
Consider how settings are presented in shape poems.

The Tornado

Swirling, twirling round and round,

2   sucking up the earth and ground.

Wind so strong and sky so black,

4   it will destroy all in its track.

Danger, danger, please beware,

6   because tornadoes

do not care.

Anonymous

Comprehension

A

Answer the questions using words from 'The Tornado'.

1 Which words at the ends of lines rhyme?

2 Which words within the same line rhyme?

3 Which words are repeated in the same line and why?

B

1 List the four verbs that describe what a tornado does.

2 How does the shape of the poem help you understand it and experience the language?

C

Write a shape poem of your own. Choose one of these topics from the unit.

Flood wave   **Volcano**   **Tornado**

1 First draw the outline of your shape poem.

2 Find some ideas below to help you.

  a *hurling* hot rocks at the sky in *noisy anger* // *dirtying the land*, covering fields with dust // pouring hot lava from *the corners of its mouth* ...

  b *racing silently* across the ocean, // *feeling* the seabed scraping along its *belly* // *rising* to greet the *tree*-lined *shore* ...

  c circling the *centre* of the *city*, // bending *trees*

Writing a personal travel recount

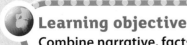
Learning objective
Combine narrative, facts and opinions into a recount.

Website pages and blogs provide **factual information**, personal **opinion** as well as **narrate** what the **writer** experienced.

The travel recount 'Expedition of a lifetime' on page 86 combines these three elements.

Model writing

1 Read the example paragraph in the box. The notes at the side show how the writer combines narrative, fact and opinion.

> ### Fighting sea lions
>
> A little further along the beach we came across a colony of sea lions, some of my favourite creatures on the island. Females gather in colonies of about 30, dominated by one bull who will aggressively defend his territory and females against other competing bulls. We saw two bull sea lions fighting. It was very noisy and bloody. We kept a safe distance, not surprisingly.

Sub-heading: Tell the reader what to expect.

Narrative progress: Say what happened next, and where.

Opinion: Adds an opinion in the middle of a sentence, or in a separate sentence.

Facts: Presents facts, usually in a present tense.

Yosemite National Park

Facts and opinions

1 Read the sentences a–h about Yosemite to get a general understanding.

2 Sort the sentences into narrative progress, opinion, and facts.

  a Apparently, the weather in Yosemite can change without warning, due to the mountainous terrain.

  b Walking further into the forest, we came to one of the three separate groves of giant sequoia trees in Yosemite.

  c We learnt that sequoia trees are the largest living things on the planet.

  d We ate our lunch in the shade of these mighty giants, as the midday sun was really hot.

  e The wildlife population includes black bears, cougars (a species of big cat), and coyotes, large wolf-like dogs that hunt in pairs.

  f Unsurprisingly, we didn't see any cougars as they are nocturnal.

  g At last, we arrived, after a long steep trek, and took our first glimpse of Yosemite Falls.

  h The views from the cliff top are spectacular and I've got some photos to prove it.

Wildlife park: Factfile

Writing frame

Write a short paragraph, combining narrative, fact, and opinion about a visit to a wildlife park. Use the Factfile and useful phrases from the boxes.

WILDLIFE PARK

Factfile

Situated:… (you decide where)

Founded: 1972

Area: covers an area of 57 hectares

Number of animals: more than 1200

Number of exotic and endangered species: 180

Species include: 93 species of mammal, including snow leopards, cheetahs, tigers

44 species of bird, including penguins, ostriches, flamingos

98 species of reptile, including chameleons, crocodiles

OPINION

- I had never seen anything so beautiful in nature before.
- While being able to do… was wonderful, what I really loved was…
- Just being able to do… was one of the most beautiful experiences of my life.
- We saw the elephants from close up, which was a beautiful sight.
- It was fun to see the penguins catch the fish in their mouths.

NARRATIVE PHRASES

- It wasn't until we arrived at the park that I realized how huge it was.
- Approaching, I got my first glimpse of the giraffes.
- The first animal we saw was…
- After lunch, we were taken to…
- Continuing on the trail, we saw many…
- As the sun began to set, we headed back to the coach.
- Soon it was getting dark and we had to leave.

Your writing

Write a recount about a visit which you made in your country to a zoo, a wildlife park, or a national park.

1 Find out information from a website and note some facts and figures. Note information about, for example, the geography, the animals and habitats.

2 Write a recount about your visit, saying:

- ▶ where you went (narrative)
- ▶ what you learnt (facts)
- ▶ what you did (narrative)
- ▶ what you thought (opinion)

Revise and check ②

Vocabulary

1 **Write the correct word for the following definitions.**

a a ruler in Ancient Egypt

b a small picture that represents a word in Egyptian writing

c information obtained by a spy

d to demand money as payment for not telling a secret

e a person who writes for people who can't write

f a tiny robot

g an instrument used to look at very small things

2 **Write the root and meaning of these words.**

valuable   solution   disappearance

3 **Complete the sentences with the correct idiom.**

to show his/her hand   to keep an eye on her

a When he was talking to the suspected spy he did not want _____

b She looked very suspicious so he decided _____

4 **Choose the correct word.**

**typhoons lava tsunami volcano hurricanes
floods earthquake tornadoes twisters**

When the ground shakes it is an (a) and if it happens in the sea it makes a big wave called a (b) which (c) the land. An erupting mountain is a (d) and hot (e) pours down the mountain. Tropical rainstorms with very strong winds are called (f) or (g). Tall spirals of wind that suck everything up are called (h) or (i).

Punctuation

1 **Put in the correct punctuation in the dialogue below.**

I feel sick said Jenna. It's your own fault cried her brother. You ate twelve chocolate brownies, you greedy girl. But you ate ten yourself said Jenna. I saw you.

2 **Write out the sentence below twice, once using dashes, once using brackets.**

James Bond the fictional spy is the hero in many books and films.

Grammar

1 Change these sentences from passive to active.

a The dinner was cooked by my grandmother.

b The visitors were frightened by the howling wolves.

c My mother was terrified by the storm.

2 Make two sentences from each word, once as a noun and once as a verb.

permit spell

3 Make adjectives from these verbs.

sleep   explode   please   talk

Spelling

1 Give two examples for each prefix.

dis– im– il– un– re–

2 Write a word for each ending.

–able   –ible   –or   –er   –ck   –k   –less   -ness

3 Add prefixes to the words in brackets to change the meaning.

Our neighbour is very (kind). He keeps our ball when it goes into his garden. It is (possible) to get it back. He is very (helpful) and (patient).

4 Spell these words correctly.

imprefect   dissappointed   unnhapy

7 Performance art

1

2

3

4

"A day without laughter is a wasted day."
Charlie Chaplin

Let's Talk

1. The pictures on these two pages show performance arts—theatre, music, dance, clowning, and acrobatics. Tell a partner about performances you have either watched or taken part in.

2. Which pictures on these page could be of a circus?

The circus

Learning objective
Structure talk to aid a listener's understanding and engagement.

Word Cloud

acrobats	clown
applause	performance
audience	ring
circus	stilts

A

Match the captions to the photographs on these two pages.

a African drummers and dancers performing on stage

b A clown paints his face before a performance

c In this old-fashioned trick, an acrobat flies out of a cannon

d A woodblock advertisement for a Japanese circus in 1845

e Zimbabwean actors in a Shakespeare play at London's Globe Theatre

> **Word origins**
> The word 'circus' was used from the 14th century, but it came from the Greek word *kirkos* meaning a 'circle' or 'ring'.

5

B

Match the words in the Word Cloud to these definitions. Then use each word in a sentence of your own.

1 a show

2 a series of acts performed by acrobats, jugglers, clowns or animals

3 people who watch or listen to a performance

4 a performer who makes people laugh

5 tall sticks on which people walk so that they look taller

6 clapping from the audience

7 the circular space where circus performers do their acts

8 people who do tricks with their bodies

Challenge

Research the history of circuses in books or on the Internet. Using your findings and the timeline below, plan a talk in chronological order (with the oldest circuses first). When you have planned it, give a talk to the class about the history of circuses.

494 BCE to 117 CE
Roman circuses built for horse races, jugglers, and acrobats

200 CE to 1800 CE
Jugglers and clowns performed in the street, but there was no special place for a circus

1919
In Russia, Lenin called circus 'the people's art form'

221 BCE to 220 CE
Chinese acrobatic performances developed

1882
Philip Astley established eight permanent circuses in Europe

2012
Contemporary circus Cirque du Soleil has workers, from 50 nationalities

Classic fiction

This text is from a famous classic written in 1938. Peter and Santa have run away to find their Uncle Gus, who works for Cobb's Circus. This is the first time they watch the show. Their friend Alexsis, a Russian acrobat, is with them.

Word Cloud

fantastic   sprinkled
immense   striding
magnificent velvet

The Circus Parade

The parade went by. There were clowns in all imaginable garments. Gus was dressed as a sailor and was striding along on immense stilts. There were horses. They wore colourful harnesses. The ponies pulled a little coach with a girl standing up in it dressed as a butterfly. The
5 six elephants were magnificent with golden cloths on their backs. They held each other by the tail. On the front one, dressed all in gold, sat a man whom the children guessed must be Kundra. There were groups of people wearing fantastic clothes. When they had gone, it was quite odd to see the ring was still sprinkled with
10 sawdust. It would not have been surprising to see that it had turned to gold...

"This is Paula," Alexsis whispered.

Paula had the same red hair as Alexsis. She was wearing a jade-green velvet tunic and cap. She was standing on the backs of
15 two of the greys. One foot on each. She rode round the ring. Then, just as she passed the entrance, in bounded a third grey. He passed under her legs and as he went she caught a silk rein looped on his back, and drove him before her. Round the three horses went until they were again past the entrance; then a fourth grey cantered in,
20 passed under her legs and was again caught and driven in front of her. Santa was terrified.

"Oh, goodness, won't she fall off?"

Alexsis laughed. "No. She have rode this since she is little."

"How many horses is she going to drive in the end?"
25 asked Peter.

"Seven," Alexsis explained. "Then there are the two she stand on. That makes nine."

The children began to count. Five. Six. They were terribly afraid she would miss
30 the ribbon on the seventh. But no, she caught it, and drove her team out amidst roars of applause.

From *Circus Shoes* by Noel Streatfeild

Comprehension

Learning objective

Comment on writer's use of language, demonstrating awareness of its impact on the reader.

Glossary

coach a carriage pulled by horses

rein a strap used by a rider to guide a horse

sawdust powder that comes from wood when it is cut with a saw

A

Copy and complete the table in note form.

People or animals	What they are wearing	What they are doing
Gus	Dressed as a sailor	
Girl in coach		
		Holding each other by the tail
Kundra		
	Dressed in a green tunic	

The author helps the reader to imagine the circus by using powerful verbs and exciting adjectives.

1 Which two verbs in the Word Cloud tell us about movement?

2 Which three adjectives make the circus sound large and exciting?

3 Find three words in the text that make the circus seem brightly coloured.

B

Writer's use of language

1 Read the second part of the text, beginning at line 22. Find one example of each of a–d.

  a The author uses some very short sentences.

  b The author shows us that Alexsis doesn't use English correctly.

  c One horse comes in at a time, so Paula's task seems extra difficult.

  d The children feel worried.

C

What about you?

If you were Santa or Peter, which circus performer would you like to be your friend? Why?

Spelling patterns

Learning objective
Continue to learn words, apply patterns and improve accuracy in spelling.

Top Tip

Writing rhyming verse can help you to remember how words with similar spellings can have different sounds.

The extract 'The Circus Parade' has words with 'ou' that have different sounds. Say these words aloud:

groups   would   round   fourth   colourful

A

1   Say these words aloud, then sort them into the correct groups, according to the 'ou' sound.

**about   bought   boulder   could   colourful
shoulder   shout   tough   your**

'or' sound	'ow' sound	'o' sound	'uh' sound
your	shout	boulder	double

The extract 'The Circus Parade' also has one word with '**au**' – 'Paula'. Words with '**au**' can have different sounds.

B

1   Which three words with 'au' letters do not have the same sound as the other words?

**applause   aunt   because   caught   cause
daughter   draught   fault   laugh   laundry
naughty   pause   saucepan**

2   Write three sentences, using as many words as you can from the list in each sentence.

Connectives

Learning objective
Use a wider range of connectives to clarify relationships between ideas.

A connective is a word or phrase that links clauses or sentences. Connectives can be:

Conjunctions *Example:* but

Subordinating connectives *Example:* although

Connecting adverb *Example:* however, finally

Connectives can be used to connect clauses within a sentence or to join up separate sentences.

A

Complete the paragraph below with the missing connectives so that there is a build-up of tension.

just   but   however   then   at first   as

_____ I inched forward, it became darker. Much darker. Too dark to see clearly. _____, I thought that if I moved slowly I could make it to the door. _____ I saw it. _____ I thought it was the sound of my own movements. _____ then it moved.

Use '**and**' and '**then**' to show the order of events.

He stood on his hands and then balanced a chair on his feet.

Use '**but**' and '**although**' to show contrast. Use '**However**' at the start of a sentence.

Although he had broken his finger, he continued his circus act.

B

Complete the beginning of the children's story 'Little Red Riding Hood' using some of the connectives.

although   and   as   as soon as   but
however   just as   because   then   until

One morning, Little Red Riding Hood was told by her mother to take a basket of food to her sick grandmother. (1) _____ she was leaving, her mother called out, "Don't go into the woods, (2) _____ the wolf will eat you!" (3) _____, Little Red Riding Hood was not afraid of wolves, that is, not (4) _____ she saw this one. (5) _____ she knew the way to Granny's house, Little Red Riding Hood went off the path...

Reading for information

Learning objective
Recognize the key characteristics of an information text.

Word Cloud

evolved   revolution
jewellery   tightrope
mime   touring
reinvented

The Reinvention of the Circus

Acrobats have performed in many countries for centuries, but in the past forty years the circus has been reinvented. Many new kinds of circus have evolved.

5 The Cirque du Soleil is French for Circus of the Sun and was founded in Canada during the 1980s. There have been 19 shows in over 270 cities on every continent except Antarctica. New shows are always being developed. Each theme-based story is told through live music, acrobats, jugglers, tightrope walkers, dancers, fire-eaters
10 and mime. Lighting and music make it very exciting. Saltimbanco, the oldest touring show, is a celebration of life to cheer us up. The costumes are all in vivid primary colours.

The modern Chinese circus began in the 1990s.
15 The Chinese State Circus, said to be the world's greatest acrobatic circus, has toured in a hundred countries. It is an example of a traditional performance art that can trace its history back to two thousand years ago, when an acrobatic display was called "the show of a hundred
20 tricks". A recent show featured jugglers, plate-spinners, a band of musicians and ten acrobats on a single bicycle.

Russian circuses have always told stories with dance. Their 2012 touring show was called The Twelve Chairs. Set in Russia in 1927, it was about a young man whose
25 grandmother revealed on her deathbed that her jewellery was hidden in one of twelve dining chairs. During the Russian revolution, the chairs were taken away. Of course, the chair was found at the end, but not before a wonderful performance with music, dance, acrobats and tightrope
30 walkers.

We do not know how circuses will develop in the future. Probably they will use more complicated technology with special lighting and sound effects. But some things will not change. People have always enjoyed
35 doing tricks with their bodies — and they always will.

Glossary

saltimbanco street acrobat or entertainer; it comes from the Italian *saltare* (jump) *in banco* (bench), which means to jump on a bench

Chinese acrobats

Cirque du Soleil

Comprehension

Learning objective
Analyse how paragraphs are structured and linked.

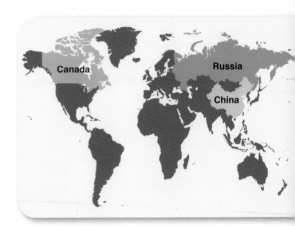

A

Copy and complete the table.

1 In the text 'The Reinvention of the Circus', three different circuses are described. Write *yes*, *no* or *don't know* in each column to complete the table with the features of each circus.

2 Add three more columns for *tightrope walkers*, *plate-spinners*, and *jugglers*.

	acrobats	dancers	fire-eaters	musicians	story-based
Cirque du Soleil					
Chinese State Circus					
Moscow State Circus					

B

Complete the sentences with the words below.

topic   paragraph   information   conclusion

1 A _____ is a group of sentences that are all about the same subject.

2 In an _____ text, like 'The Reinvention of the Circus', a new paragraph is shown by leaving out a line.

3 The _____ sentence in each paragraph tells the reader what the paragraph is about.

4 The final paragraph ties up the text in a _____ .

C

Invent a subheading for each paragraph of the extract text.

Discussion time

Imagine you have to organize a new kind of circus which is made up of modern day acts, such as mountain bike stunts. In a group, decide on which acts you would like to include and why they should be included. Present your ideas to the rest of the class.

Acrobats from The Moscow State Circus

Prefixes and suffixes

> ### Learning objective
> Know how to transform meaning with prefixes and suffixes.

Remember: A **prefix** is a group of letters added to the beginning of a word to change the meaning. *Example:* 're–' means 'again'. So 're–' + 'invent' means 'invent again'.

Remember: A **suffix** is a group of letters added to the end of a word to change the meaning. *Example:* '–wise' means 'in a certain direction'. So 'clock' + '–wise' means 'in the direction of the hands on a clock'.

A

Match the prefixes on the left with their meanings.

1 underestimate	**a** again
2 oversleep	**b** in the opposite way
3 retell	**c** too little
4 unwind	**d** too much

B

Complete the sentences using suitable words with the prefixes in **A** and these root forms.

1 I think the waiter has under _____ us. He's forgotten to add the ice creams to our bill.

2 The result was a 3–3 draw, so the teams will have to re _____ the match.

3 There's no need to re _____ and get angry. I was only joking.

C

Create suitable words for the sentences below by adding a prefix and suffix to a root word.

Prefixes and suffixes

un ing re able ment over

Root words

imagine   develop   eat

1 _____ is unhealthy and makes one fat.

2 Many houses needed _____ after the destruction caused by the hurricane.

3 Nobody tidied up after the picnic. The mess was _____ .

Using commas

Learning objective
Develop increasing accuracy in using punctuation effectively
to mark out the meaning in complex sentences.

▶ Complex sentences are made up of one **important clause** (main clause) and
a **less important** clause (subordinate clause). Every clause contains a verb.

▶ You can join clauses together with '**or**', '**and**' or '**but**'. Use commas unless the
sentences are very short.

Examples: *You could go to the library and borrow a guide book about Turkey, or
you could do an Internet search.*

She entered the room and sat down.

▶ Subordinate clauses begin with words like 'if', 'when', 'as'.

When less important clauses come first, they are usually followed by commas.
When main clauses come first, they are not followed by commas.

Examples: *If you get the chance when you're in the capital, go and see the circus.*
Don't phone me when you arrive as I'll be asleep.

A

Read the sentences below and decide whether or not a comma is
needed. Where would you put it?

1 If you want to learn to ride a horse I'll pay for some riding lessons.

2 Aunt Lucy phoned you but didn't leave a message.

3 I had fish soup a steak and chips and Kate had spaghetti a salad and
an ice cream.

4 The keeper asked what we were doing and I said that we were
looking for the elephant house.

Relative clauses are introduced by words like '**who**', '**which**', '**that**'.

Non-identifying relative clauses do not identify people or things; they simply give us
more information. Commas must be used in these clauses.

I saw two police officers, who were wearing bright yellow jackets.

B

Read the sentences and decide how many commas should be added.

1 I looked through my binoculars and saw a very large cat that looked
like a lion.

2 We are staying at the Grand Hotel which has a heated swimming pool.

Dragon performance

Learning objective
Analyse the success of writing in evoking particular moods.

During Chinese New Year celebrations, performers take on the costume of a dragon or lion and dance through the streets.

Dragon Dance

A Chinese dragon's in the street
And dancing on its Chinese feet
With fearsome head and golden scale
And twisting its ferocious tail.
5 Its bulging eyes are blazing red
While smoke is puffing from its head
And well you nervously might ask
What lies behind that fearful mask.
It twists and twirls across the road
10 While BANG the cracker strings explode.
Don't yell or run or shout or squeal
Or make a Chinese dragon's meal
For, where its heated breath is fired
They say it likes to be admired.
15 With slippered joy and prancing shoe
Why, you can join the dragon too.
There's fun with beating gongs and din
When dragons dance the New Year in.

Max Fatchen

Comprehension

Learning objective

Discuss and express preferences in terms of language, style and theme.

Word Cloud

bulging   puffing

din   scale

prancing

A

Give evidence from the poem to support your answers.

1 What performance is the poet describing?

2 What time of year does this performance take place?

3 Why would the reader be nervous in line 7?

B

Poet's use of language

1 The poet uses powerful adjectives to describe the dragon:

- ▶ fearsome
- ▶ golden
- ▶ ferocious
- ▶ bulging eyes are blazing red

Suggest adjective synonyms for these four phrases.

2 What effect do the rhyming verses have on the rhythm of the poem?

3 Why does the poet make the verses rhyme and have this rhythm?

4 Which theme do you think is the most important within the poem?

   a excitement

   b fear

   c celebration

C

What about you?

1 Do you like the poem? Give examples from the poem to explain your feelings about it.

2 Would you like to take part in a dragon dance? Explain why or why not.

107

For or against?

Learning objective
Argue a case in writing, developing points logically and convincingly.

When we write an argument, we have to:
- decide whether we are **for** or **against** an idea
- present **opinions** clearly and in a **logical order**
- give **evidence** or tell a true story to support our point of view
- **persuade** the reader to accept our view.

Model writing

Read these two letters to a newspaper. Which letter is for allowing animals to perform in a circus? Which letter is against? Use the phrases in blue from the first letter to help you complete the second letter.

LETTER 1

I am writing to express my outrage that animals were performing at the circus in West Park. In my view, animals should not be allowed to perform in circuses.

Wild animals like elephants, monkeys and tigers should live in their natural habitat, which is the jungle. It was clear that the performing animals were unhappy. **For example**, the monkey seemed to be crying while it was rolling a hoop across the ring. **In my opinion**, we should set circus animals free.

Secondly, the trainers are beating the animals to make them do tricks. I know this fact because there was an elephant with a wound on its side while it was dancing. Its rider was hitting it with a stick in the very same place. **In addition**, the Animal Protection Society claims that three quarters of circus animals are cruelly treated.

In conclusion, if any readers are thinking of buying tickets for the circus next week, I urge them to think again. If you want to see wild animals, go to a wildlife park, not to a circus.

Yours faithfully,

J Gomez

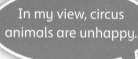

In my view, circus animals are unhappy.

I disagree. Circus animals enjoy performing.

LETTER 2

_____ support for allowing animals to perform in circuses. _____, animals love to please people and enjoy doing tricks.

Many of these animals were not born in the jungle but reared by loving trainers. They would not know how to survive in the jungle – they would probably get eaten by other animals. _____, some animals would not be alive if they were not in the circus. _____, tigers are endangered because their jungle habitats are being cut down.

_____, there is no harm in keeping circus animals so long as their owners look after them properly.

_____

Kiran Grover

Writing frame

Should children be television stars? Below is a list of arguments for and against. Which are phrases for and which are against?

Child stars grow up too fast.

Child stars can earn a lot of money.

They miss school, so get bad exam results.

They often become stars in later life.

They can become big-headed and greedy.

They meet a lot of interesting people.

Your writing

Write a letter to a newspaper arguing for or against allowing children to perform on TV and become television stars.

In each paragraph, state your point of view in the first sentence and then support it with an example, story or evidence. Follow this plan, using some of the given phrases.

Genevieve Hannelius stars as Avery in *Dog with a Blog* on the Disney Channel.

Introduction	I am writing to … In my view, … In my opinion, … Here are my reasons:	
First point	Firstly, … To begin with, …	For example, I know this because …
Further points	Secondly, … Thirdly, …	
		In addition, … Moreover, … What is more, …
Conclusion	In conclusion, … Finally, …	
Signing off	Yours faithfully, …	

8 Let's celebrate!

Let's Talk

1 Celebrations and festivals often include: special food, music, lights, singing and dancing, different clothes, fireworks, and crowds. Find these in the pictures above.

2 Which of the celebrations in the pictures would you like to be involved in?

3 Give three reasons why people have celebrations.

4 What festivals do you have in your country?

"Celebration is a kind of food we all need in our lives, and each individual brings a special recipe or offering, so that together we will make a great feast."
Corita Kent and Jan Steward

The world loves to celebrate

Learning objective
Structure talk to aid a listener's understanding and engagement.

Word Cloud

anniversary	feast
carnival	fireworks
commemorate	float
confectionary	harvest
custom	parade
decoration	

A

Match the illustrations on the opposite page with the sentences below.

A They celebrated the harvest with a musical performance.

B The decoration on the first float in the parade was spectacular.

C The family commemorated the day with the a birthday cake.

D They celebrated New Year's Day with a firework display.

B

Solve the word puzzles below.

1 A f _ _ _ _ is a delicious meal with lots of different food that lasts for days.

2 Match the words to the correct word class description.

celebrate	decorate	noun
celebrated	decorated	verb
celebration	decoration	past participle verb

3 Unscramble the words and match them to their definition.

skorwerif	A celebration or party held at the same time each year
narcilav	Loud colourful explosions
varsinneray	A large, lively parade which moves through a town or city

Kwaanza is an African-American celebration.

C

Prepare a talk about your favourite festival or celebration and present it to the class. Use the points below to help you.

▶ Name the celebration in your introduction.

▶ List its celebratory features, such as rest from work, chance for families to meet.

▶ Next give details of the celebration, including the dates and places.

▶ Finish with sentences on why a visitor might want to observe this celebration and why it is your favourite.

Preparing for Chinese New Year

Learning objective
Consider how the author manipulates the reaction of the reader and how characters and settings are presented.

Word Cloud

boast   nudged
flipped   smirk
meanest

This extract comes from a story about an eight-year-old boy – Artie – growing up in Chinatown, in San Francisco. His family have gathered together for a celebration.

A Ridiculous Promise

Our parties weren't much fun for me. I was the youngest and the smallest. So I was never smart enough or strong enough to win any game. That was frustrating. And then my older brother, Harry, and my cousins always rubbed it in. That made me feel even worse. The meanest cousin was Petey...

5   Petey needled me every chance he got.

After Artie loses a game of Monopoly to Petey all the cousins start discussing fireworks...

Petey dismissed me with a wave of his hand. "What would you know about firecrackers, shrimp? All you do is watch with Granny."

10   "I'll show you," I said. "This year, I'll have my own firecrackers."
I was so mad that I didn't stop to think. "I'll have so many, I'll... give them away."...

"When you're twenty?" Petey asked.

Harry nudged me, "Don't let Petey egg you on like this."

I should have listened to Harry's warnings. All I could see was Petey's 15 smirk though.

"This Chinese New Year's," I said.

I didn't know when that was. The American year was based on the sun. The Chinese year was based on the moon. They didn't match. I went to the calendar in the kitchen. Mom was making tea.

20   "When is Chinese New Year's?" I asked her. I flipped through the pages. I didn't see it in there. I was disappointed.

"You won't find it in an American calendar," Mom explained.

She checked a small Chinese calendar that Granny had given her.

25   "It's February third." She added, "It'll be the Year of the Horse."

Things got worse when we went to school. Petey told everyone about my boast. If I didn't give firecrackers to my family, all my friends would know.

from *The Star Maker* by Laurence Yep

Comprehension

A

Use words and phrases from the extract to support your answers.

1 Which two statements about Artie are false?

   a He enjoys family celebrations.

   b He is old enough to attend school.

   c He knows a lot about the Chinese New Year.

   d He wants to prove himself to his cousins.

2 As a Chinese boy growing up in America, Artie is in between two different cultures. What is the main difference between the American and Chinese calendars?

3 Find a quotation in the extract that shows Harry tries to help Artie.

B

Writer's use of language

1 Throughout the extract, the writer conveys the range and strength of Artie's feelings. Find a word or phrase in the text which shows that he is:

   a annoyed

   b furious

   c upset

2 Do you feel sorry for Artie? Explain your answer and use phrases from the extract to support your reason.

C

Look at the words below. Match the New Year greeting with the correct language. You can look the phrases up on the Internet.

"Gung Hay Fat Choy" Hawaiian

Chinese "Hauoli Makahiki Hou"

"Gutes Neues Jahr" Polish

Tagalog (Philippines) "Bonne Année"

German "Maligayang Bagong Taon"

"Yeni Yılınız Kutlu Olsun" French

Turkish "Szczęśliwego nowego"

The Chinese calendar

Glossary

Chinese calendar a calendar based on the cycles of the moon

firecrackers fireworks that make a loud explosive noise. They are often part of Chinese New Year celebrations

needled deliberately and continuously annoyed

shrimp a small shellfish, but sometimes used as an insult to mean 'little'

Proverbs and idioms

 Learning objective
Explore proverbs, sayings and figurative expressions.

The extract 'A Ridiculous Promise' contains some popular sayings and figurative expressions. The writer has used them to make the story seem more realistic.

A

1 Find these expressions in the text and rewrite them in formal English. Your 'translations' should make sense within the sentence.

rubbed it in

what would you know about firecrackers

shrimp

don't let him egg you on like this

2 English expressions or idioms are used when people are speaking informally to one another. Match the idiom to the correct phrase.

off the top of your head	to be honest about your opinion
on the tip of your tongue	get to the point
speak your mind	from the very beginning
from scratch	say something without thinking about it beforehand
cut a long story short	you know the word, but cannot quite remember it for a minute

A **proverb** is an expression that gives wise advice.

Example: 'All that glitters is not gold' means things aren't as valuable as they might seem.

B

Read the three proverbs from different countries. Choose one that you like. Write it out and draw an illustration to show what it means.

India: Give a man a fish and you feed him for a day; teach a man to fish and you feed him for a lifetime. (Give people skills and education so that they can be independent.)

Finland: Even a small star shines in the darkness. (Everything has its worth.)

Egypt: A beautiful thing is never perfect. (Something can still be beautiful and not perfect.)

> ⋯ **Challenge** ⋯
> Find out about three proverbs commonly used in your own culture. You could ask your family and friends for examples.

Formal and informal language

Learning objective
Understand the conventions of standard English usage in different forms of writing.

Standard English is the form of English used in writing and in formal speaking situations. **Non-standard English** is often used in more informal, spoken situations – between friends or family. It uses different grammar and contains idiomatic phrases.

A

Read the extract from *Tom Sawyer* by Mark Twain, set in the American South. Tom has been told to whitewash (paint) his aunt's garden fence.

Replace the blue text with standard English.

"*Say*, Tom, let ME whitewash a little."

Tom considered, was about to consent; but he altered his mind:

"No – no – I reckon it would hardly do, Ben. You see, Aunt Polly's awful particular about this fence – right here on the street, you know – it's got to be done very careful; I reckon there ain't one boy in a thousand, maybe two thousand, that can do it the way it's gotta be done."

B

1   Complete the table with the standard English phrases.

Common 'errors'	Non-standard English	Standard English
Double negatives	I don't want no ice cream.	
Mix-up with irregular verbs	I swimmed across the sea.	
Incorrect use of pronouns	Pass them sweets.	
Mix-up between 'well' and 'good'	The boy played good.	
Forgetting to add –ly to adverbs	He spoke loud.	
Slang vocabulary and shortened words	Yeah, ain't, guys, cool, reckon, 'cos	

2   Change the non-standard English in blue to standard English.

Hey, guys! I'm cool. Yeah, I reckon our party is gonna be the best 'cos we got loads of real good food.

Trung Thu, a Vietnamese festival

Learning objective
Compare the language, style and impact of a range of non-fiction writing.

Van Prepares for the Festival

Originally, Trung Thu came about as a way for parents to make up for lost time with their children after the harvest season.

How people enjoy Trung Thu

Van is twelve years old and lives in Vietnam. Each year she joins
5 hordes of other children who go out into the streets with glowing lanterns to enjoy Trung.

This mid-autumn festival celebrates the beauty of the moon, which is brighter and whiter than at any other time of year. The festival involves a family gathering where parents spoil their children
10 with treats and tasty moon cakes.

Trung Thu masks

Van and her friends enjoy wearing masks on Trung Thu. In the past children made their own masks, but today they buy them. Colourful masks are dotted around the shops on Hang
15 Ma Street, which sell a wonderful variety of plastic and papier-mâché masks.

Moon cakes

On nearly every street corner, there are stalls selling fish and flower-shaped moon cakes. Moon cakes are a traditional part
20 of the Trung Thu festivities and come in two varieties. Bánh Deo is unbaked, white and sticky, and Bánh Nuong is brown and baked. Moon cakes contain unusual fillings, such as sugar with meat or eggs.

from Celebration! Celebration! (Children Just Like Me) by Anabel Kindersley

Word Cloud
dotted
hordes
stalls
treats
unbaked

On Trung Thu, the moon looks like a yellow ball, full and beautiful. My mother buys me moon cakes and I arrange them on a tray with some fruit. We eat them on the terrace. Then I put a candle inside my star lantern, light it and go outside to meet my friends and follow the procession through the streets.

Comprehension

A

Read the passage about Trung Thu and choose the correct answers.

1 Trung Thu is a mid-autumn festival celebrating

  a growing-up   **b** the moon   **c** birthdays

2 The children go out into the streets with

  a lanterns   **b** firecrackers   **c** kites

3 During this festival the parents spoil their children with

  a new clothes   **b** tasty treats   **c** books and paints

4 Moon cakes contain unusual fillings such as

  a fish with chocolate   **b** potato and fruit   **c** meat and sugar

5 The stalls in the street sell

  a colourful masks   **b** olive oil   **c** recipe books

Vietnam

B

What do you think?

1 Why have the subheadings been used? Choose one answer.

  a To tell the reader what each paragraph is about

  b To help the reader understand the text

  c To make the text more interesting

  d To give the main ideas

2 'Van Prepares for the Festival' is a non-fiction text, so its purpose is to give facts and information. Write down six facts you have found out from the extract.

3 If non-fiction texts were all facts, they could be uninteresting for readers. What two personal features has the writer included to make the text more appealing to the reader?

Glossary

moon cakes small cakes traditionally eaten during the mid-autumn festivities in various parts of Asia

papier-mâché paper mixed with glue or flour and water; used for making ornaments

spoil to give a child everything they ask for in a way that has a bad effect on their behaviour

C

Summarize the Trung Thu festival in 100 words for a book on celebrations around the world. Include personal opinions as well as facts.

Discussion time

'Old, traditional festivals are out of date.' Do you agree or disagree with this statement? Find out more about some traditional festivals and use your research as evidence to support your opinion.

Connectives

Learning objective
Use connectives to structure an argument or discussion.

In writing, **connectives** are very important in helping the reader to follow points and ideas.

A

Complete the sentences below with one of the following words.

although   before   however   when   since   while   during

a _____ he was a good sportsman, Juan was not good at basketball.

b _____ he has had a new teacher, he has quickly improved.

c _____ her time at junior school, she played in many tennis matches.

d _____ she moved to Hong Kong, Anya had not celebrated Chinese New Year.

B

1 It is important that the right type of connective is used. Choose five connectives from below and insert them in the right spaces in the paragraph.

However	Firstly	On the other hand	Secondly	Also

Similarly	In the same way	Next	Finally	Lastly	If

_____ I would like to make the point that celebrations make people feel happier. _____ there were no celebrations, the world would be a very dull place. _____, if there were too many celebrations, no work would get done! _____ if celebrations last too long, they can get in the way of daily life. _____ I would like to make a plea that we do not lose our celebrations across the world. They are very important!

2 Read through your text to check it makes sense.

C

Write a paragraph arguing why a particular celebration in your culture is important. Use as many connectives as you can from the exercise above to help you link and connect your points.

Difficult words and homophones

Learning objective
Continue to learn words, apply patterns, and improve accuracy in spelling.

To ensure that your spelling is of a high standard, you will need to continue to use strategies to help you remember words.

A

Choose ten words from the Tricky Spellings that you find difficult to spell. Use these strategies to help you remember them.

▸ Look, say, cover, write, check: *look* at the word; *say* it, exaggerating any difficult letters; *cover* it; *write* it; then *check* it.

▸ Write the word out over and over again, highlighting or making bigger the letters that are difficult to remember.

▸ Break it into affixes (prefix, root word, suffix).
Example: un-fortunate-ly

▸ Break it into syllables. *Example:* re-mem-ber

▸ Break it into phonemes. *Example:* di-a-ry

▸ Find a word within a word. *Example:* fav-OUR-ite

Tricky Spelling

accommodation
actually
argument
beautiful
beginning
believe
caught
definite
disappear
disappoint

embarrass
happened
height
necessary
queue
remember
shoulder
strength

B

Homophones are words that sound the same and are difficult to spell. You need to use strategies to help you learn them.

Words	Strategies
cloth/clothe	They sound different: 'cloth' sounds like it spells, whereas 'clothe' has an 'e' on the end, making the 'o' sound different, like 'oh!'
passed/past	'I passed her by': 'passed' is a verb, so is important in a sentence, and longer than 'past', which comes after the verb, such as: 'I walked past the man'.
practice/practise	'practice' is a noun: 'I go for a drum practice'; 'practise' is a verb: 'I am going to practise my drumming'. They should go in different places in a sentence.

Work out strategies for remembering the following pairs.

board/bored	currant/current	desert/dessert
hoarse/horse	**principle/principal**	**stationery/stationary**

Celebrating nature

Learning objective
Comment on the writer's use of language, demonstrating awareness of its impact on the reader.

Word Cloud

caverns   relic
flourish   tribute
freaks

The Boab tree of North-West Australia is a relative of the Baobab trees of Africa. These trees have huge trunks and often have hollows, like huge caverns, inside them.

The week-long Boab Festival starts at the end of July each year in Western Australia.

Tree Festival

On the landscapes of Australia
  the weirdest shapes appear,
  so many freaks of nature
  that only flourish here.
There's one found in the north-west,
5 no odder sight you'll see:
  a relic of the Dreamtime
  is the mighty Boab tree.
Out near the Fitroy River
  a grim old tale they tell,
10 how one great hollow Boab
  became a prison cell.
But now, when wattle's blooming,
  each year the people throng
  to join the Boab Festival,
15 for sport and dance and song,
And some will hold their picnics
  near a tribe's Corroboree –
  it's like a kind of tribute
  to the mighty Boab tree.

David Bateson

Comprehension

A

Use words and phrases from the poem to support your answers.

1 The Boab tree is now used for celebrations, but the poet suggests that it had an ugly past. Find three phrases which show this.

2 Find four words or phrases in the poem that are to do with celebration.

3 Find a word in the poem that tells us that large crowds gather at the Festival.

4 The poet refers to 'a grim old tale they tell' but doesn't tell the reader what this is. What do you think could have happened?

Glossary

Corroboree a dance held by Aboriginal Australians at times of festivity or at times of war

the Dreamtime the set of beliefs of Aboriginal Australians

wattle an Australian tree with a bright yellow flower

B

What do you think?

1 Why do you think the poet uses the word 'mighty' to describe the tree?

2 The poem starts off in a depressing way, then changes to be more cheerful and celebratory. Which two words signal this change?

C

What about you?

Which natural place near where you live (such as a park, forest, desert, river, lake or sea, or mountain) would be a good place to hold a new festival, and why?

The golden wattle is the national flower of Australia.

Writing instructions

 Learning objective
Adapt the conventions of the text type for a particular purpose.

Instructions and explanations are closely related. An instruction describes how something is done, step by step. An explanation explains how something works – the underlying processes involved. Both answer the questions 'How?' and 'Why?' but very differently because they have different purposes.

Model writing

Look at the instructions for making a lantern. Note the key features.

A Purpose Make sure this is clear.

Making lanterns for a festival

B Material needed usually appears as a list of items

You will need:

- Balloons
- Empty bowls
- Tissue paper (white and bright colours)
- Glue
- Wool
- Battery-operated tea lights

C Method: arranged in chronological order and often numbered

D Adverbs used

1 Place the blown-up balloon in an empty bowl. Use the glue to paste the white tissue over the bottom part of the blown-up balloons.

2 **Leave** to dry overnight.

3 Repeat the process with brightly coloured tissues.

Again leave to dry in a cool place.

4 Cut the balloons out as in the picture below.

5 Punch four holes along the edge. String the wool through the holes and attach to sticks for carrying.

6 **Carefully** insert a small battery-operated tea light in each balloon.

Use as decorations for parties or festivals.

E Commands used and most sentences start with a verb

F Ends with a conclusion or suggested use of the product

Instructions to make a kite

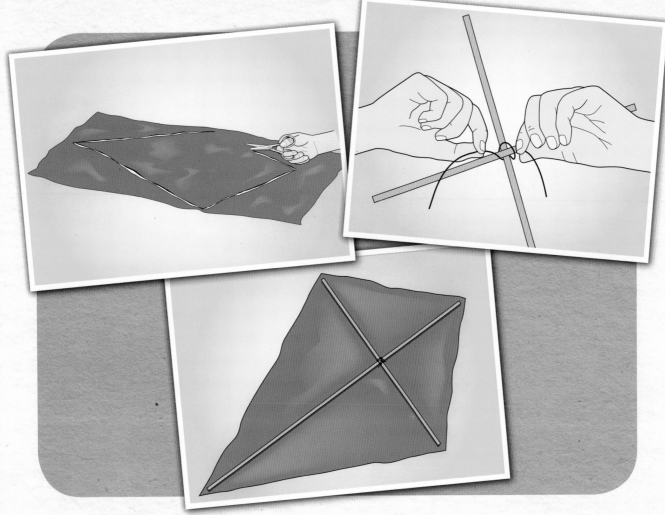

Write your own instructions for making a kite

1 Put the numbers of the pictures in the right order to make clear instructions for making a kite.

2 Write the instructions for making a kite following the model on page 122. The list of materials has already been done for you.

You will need:

▸ A large plastic rubbish bag (about 50 litres capacity)

▸ Two wooden dowels or straight sticks, one 60 centimetres long, the other 20–50 centimetres long.

▸ Scissors

▸ String or fishing line

▸ Ruler

▸ Clear sticky packing tape

▸ Ribbon and permanent markers for additional decoration

Challenge

Choose a recipe, a decoration, or a costume for a festival. Write either an explanation or an instruction to say how it is made.

9 Media mayhem

Aunt and Uncle just had a baby boy. All well.

"The things most people want to know about are usually none of their business."

George Bernard Shaw

Let's Talk

1 Where do you get news and information? Use the photos on this page for some ideas.

2 Do you think we get too much news? Why?

Information overload

Learning objective
Structure talk to aid a listener's understanding and engagement.

Word Cloud
blog
communication
media
overload
privacy

A

1 How many different ways do you or your family get news or information?

2 How do you think you'll get news in the future? Can you think of a new way?

B

Read the notes below and prepare to give a short talk to the class about information overload.

1 Today we live in a multi-media world. The term, media, used to mean TV, radio, newspapers, and magazines. But now we can get our news, information, and entertainment in all sorts of ways, such as through smart phones with apps.

2 People can also keep in touch through social media websites.

3 Television news is updated as it happens, twenty-four hours a day, seven days a week. We can read newspapers on paper, on the Internet, or on phones or tablet computers.

4 We learn about world events as they happen because people send images from their phones.

5 Famous people are pursued by paparazzi—photographers—who sell pictures and information to the media.

6 Although it is exciting, there is a danger that we can suffer from information overload.

7 We cannot always be sure that what we see or hear is true. It may be the opinion of the person who is writing or taking the photograph.

Glossary

apps software applications which can be downloaded onto multi-media devices

multi-media the use of sound, text and film as well as the printed word

paparazzi an Italian word for photographers who chase after celebrities

social media a collective term for communication by text, instant messaging, blogs and email

C

1 Many children now communicate through mobile phones. What are the advantages and disadvantages of these?

2 Outside school, where do you get most of your information from—family, friends, television, newspapers, or magazines?

Paparazzi

Skate School on television

Learning objective
Look for implicit meanings, and make plausible inferences based on more than one point in the text.

The children at Skate School, a sports boarding school, are training for the World Skating Championships. Then they are told that they are going to be filmed for a reality TV show, *Skate School*.

Word Cloud

advertise   guidelines
capture   propelled
cropped   reassured
discreet   restricted
distracting   rink
glitziest

Adam Explains

"Students, teachers, staff..." said Madame. "In a few months, we are *all* going to be starring in a weekly reality TV show." The coaching director heaved a sigh. It was clear that this wasn't something that she was too thrilled about.

5   "But the film crew has agreed to stay within strict guidelines. Instead of following you around like the *paparazzi*, I've been assured that filming will be from a polite distance in the style of...what was it you said, Adam?"

"A fly-on-the-wall documentary," said Adam. "That way, we'll
10 capture a real sense of the wonder of figure-skating!"

"They won't be allowed into the bedrooms, will they?" asked Anushka, a popular pair skater, who was partnered with Edward and had won silver at Perfect Pairs.

"Certainly not," snapped Madame. "The film crew is
15 restricted to three main areas: the rink, the canteen and the common room. Anywhere else is strictly forbidden."

"And what if I fall over on the ice?" asked Pippa, a petite girl with cropped blonde hair and brown eyes. "I don't want to look an idiot on national television."

20   "We'll only screen it if it's a really spectacular wipe-out," promised Adam, as if that was something to be proud of. "And we'll show your best jumps too!"

Pippa didn't look reassured.

"Surely we're not here to advertise figure-skating?"
25 said a frowning Dylan. "Aren't we here to skate for Team GB? And isn't it going to be distracting having video cameras following our every move? What if our training suffers?"

"Calm down," said Adam, getting to his feet again. "We're going to create so much buzz and excitement about figure-skating that you'll be propelled into the big league. You'll be stars. Megastars. Everyone will want to be you. How *totally awesome* is that?" He smiled broadly, his Hollywood-white teeth easily the glitziest things in the canteen. "That's our job... to record everyday life at the world's coolest boarding school. We'll be so discreet, you won't even know we're here."

From *Skate School* by Kay Woodward

Glossary

common room room in school or college where everybody can meet

figure-skating skating technical patterns on ice

fly-on-the-wall imagining watching somebody without them knowing that you are there

petite French for 'very small'

reality TV a show where ordinary people take part

the big league an important person or team (a phrase used in football)

wipe-out a surfing term, used when a big wave knocks you off your surfboard

Comprehension

A

Explain your answers using words and phrases from the text.

1 Read the statements about the story. Which three are false?

   a Madame is thrilled to be in a reality TV show.

   b The film crew cannot film wherever they like.

   c Dylan is happy about being filmed.

   d Pippa does not want to look stupid on TV.

   e Adam cares about Skate School and only wants to show the best.

B

What do you think?

1 Think of three reasons why filming Skate School might be a bad idea.

2 What do you think the TV crew might say in response to each of your three concerns?

3 What do you think about Adam when he says to Pippa, "We'll only screen it if it's a really spectacular wipe-out"? Do you think he is sincere? Why or why not?

C

What about you?

1 Would you have let Adam film you if you went to Skate School? Give reasons for your answer.

2 Choose one of the students in the extract, and write their diary or blog entry on the day they hear the news of the reality TV show.

Challenge

Imagine a fly-on-the-wall documentary was made of your school.

Think of three things they could do to make your school look good on the show.

Think of three things the film-makers could do to make your school look bad on the show.

Words, old and new

Learning objective
Explore word origins and derivations and the use of words from other languages.

The fiction extract 'Adam Explains' is from a modern text and set in England, yet much of the language used is based on older words from other countries!

Example: 'advertise' comes from the 15th century French word *avertissement*.

A

Match up the words from the text with the correct derivation.

petite	From the Latin *spectaculum* (a show, spectacle) and *spectare* (to view, watch)
idiot	From the Italian *pappataci* (a small mosquito)
spectacular	From the Greek *idiwtes*
filming	From the Old English, *filmen* (a thin skin)
paparazzi	From the French *petit* (little)

B

Find out which country the following words derive from. To help you, use an etymological dictionary – you can find one on the Internet.

iceberg	average	guitar	sofa
bangle	luck	ketchup	umbrella
bamboo	hamster	orchestra	wrong

C

Words are added to the English language all the time. These words have been recently added to the *Oxford English Dictionary*. Write out their definitions.

texting   blog   hoody   wannabe   wifi   jeggings

A changing language

Not only are new words being added to the dictionary, but they can change their meaning.

Example: 'silly' once meant 'happy'!

Changes in language over time like this are due to the arrival of other languages. Sometimes slang words become accepted as normal, too.

A

You will need to use a dictionary to help you answer these questions.

1   What word beginning with 'pre' originally meant 'crafty' or 'sly'?
2   The original meaning of the word 'brave' was completely opposite to what it is now. What was it?
3   Who would have been called 'girls' in the past?
4   What is the connection between the words 'knight' and 'boy'?
5   Originally, the word 'awful' meant 'full of awe', and was used to describe something wonderful, delightful or amazing. What does it mean now?

Some new words are formed by blending – that is, by merging the sounds and meanings of two or more other words or word parts.

Example: glimmer = gleam and shimmer

B

Complete the following table of blend formations. The first has been done for you.

pulse	quasar	**pulsar**
situation	comedy	
	drama	docudrama
	magazine	fanzine
camera		camcorder

C

Words can also extend their meaning, by simply adding another meaning! Using a dictionary find out the different definitions of:

spam   virus   cell   green   garage

Investigate adverts

Word Cloud

advertisements   product
buyers   puzzles
festival   teen
persuasion

On Sale Now!

Advertisements in magazines, on television, through the post or on hoardings use the language of persuasion and bright colourful images to attract attention from buyers.

5 **Fabulous fashion**

Nearly everyone wants to be fashionable and pages like this, in teen magazines, are aimed at getting young girls to buy all the 'latest fashions'. Well-known celebrities and models
10 show off the clothes. This article uses captions such as 'so cool' and 'rocks the festival look' to show that they are up-to-the-minute and you can be, too.

These adverts have been written to
15 appeal to girls, while the adverts for boys are more likely to be for the latest console or computer game.

FASHION ● FASHION ● FASHIO

ST★R STYL

Cool shades give you star style

Complete the loo with sparkle earrir

Stand out from the crowd with cute animal prints.

Red is hot right now

Must have heels this season

Exciting games

20 This page from the Internet makes the game sound fun and exciting. It describes a game in which the characters have to use their amazing abilities. The players meet on a blue and green planet scattered with individual plots. There are 25 places to explore, items to collect and puzzles to solve. The game can be shared with other players around the world.

LittleBIGPlanet

If you were to stand on LittleBigPlanet and try to imagine a more astounding, fantastic, and creative place, full of enthralling adventure, uncanny characters, and brilliant things to do... you couldn't. All imagination is here, and what you do with it all is entirely up to you.

Build new levels and expand the environment, collect the many and varied tools and objects to make your mark on this world, or just simply enjoy the people and puzzles they've set.

Comprehension

> **Learning objective**
> Compare the language, style, and impact of a range of non-fiction writing.

Glossary

hoardings advertising boards in public places

up-to-the-minute the latest thing

A

Give evidence from the pictures to support answers to A and B.

1 Looking at the page from the girls' magazine, name two things about the layout that you think work well and two that don't. The layout will include the images used, their size, the number of them and where they are positioned.

2 Find four adjectives about Little Big Planet that help to make the game sound exciting. *Example*: brilliant

B

What do you think?

1 Does the look of the 'Star Style' page appeal to you? Why or why not?

2 Do the words , colours, images, and layout of the page used in *Little Big Planet* convince you that it is a good game?

C

How about you?

What advertisements have persuaded you—or your family—to buy something? Was the product as good as the advertisement said it was?

Discussion time

'Young people shouldn't be persuaded by adverts to buy computer and mobile phone games. They are addictive and expensive.' Explain why you agree or disagree with this opinion.

Persuasive language

Learning objective
Revise language conventions and grammatical features of different types of texts.

Read the language and grammar techniques that are used for persuasive purposes.

- use of **personal pronouns**, so the reader thinks the advert is directly addressed to them. *Example:* We will do all the hard work for you!

- **short sentences** for impact. *Example:* It's so easy.

- use of **'and'** and '**but**' to make points seem straightforward and honest. *Example:* And, what's more...

- **apostrophes for omission**, creating a conversational tone. *Example:* You couldn't ask for better.

- **adverbs** for emphasis. *Examples:* simply, naturally, only, just

- **adjectives** to describe the selling point of the product. *Example:* stupendous, brilliant, best, cheapest

- **rhetorical questions**. *Example:* Unhappy with your broadband provider?

- **connectives** that are used to prove something is correct. *Examples:* in fact, of course

- **alliteration**, so that attention is drawn to words. *Example:* better broadband

- **modal verbs**, such as 'will', 'can' and 'could', emphasizing what will be achieved. *Example:* We will change your life!

A

1 Find one example of each of the features listed above in the advertisement for broadband Internet connection.

2 Can you find other techniques used to persuade?

B

Advertisements also use layout and presentation to help persuade. Copy out the advertisement, changing the font and layout to make it more persuasive.

C

Make up an advertisement for a new brand of trainers or a computer game. Use a range of language and layout techniques!

Want to cut your broadband bills, but can't find the time because you're too busy?

- Well, just leave it to us and we will find the best deal for you. It's as easy as that!
- Simply call us free on 0800 212 212

What difference can we make?

- Top experts brought in to search the best deals for your area
- Fantastic reduction in costs

P.S. And if you don't have time today, just do it tomorrow. We will still be there. Of course, we will. Because we care...

Persuasive punctuation

Learning objective
Identify uses of the colon, semicolon, parenthetic commas, dashes and brackets.

Persuasive texts, such as advertisements, use a wide range of punctuation – often to make the text seem like a speaking voice.

Examples: You know it makes sense! Want to try a different kind of computer game?

A

Match the examples below with the correct punctuation mark.

Worried about your spots?	exclamation mark
We think (and we know we're right) that you will notice a difference.	semicolon
No more bills!	question mark
No more unhappy wash days; no more dirty shirts.	parenthetic commas
Our service, which is second to none, will change your life forever.	brackets

Advertisements sometimes use ellipses, which are three dots (no more), and look like this: ...

An ellipsis is used to show that words (or one word) have been intentionally left out.

Example: Just think about it...

B

Add an ellipsis to the end of the following sentences, and note the effect.

 With free entry for kids, it's the perfect time to try it out.

 Visit your local store today.

C

Look at the advertisement you created for C, on page 132. Add a range of punctuation so that you get the effect of a speaking voice.

Ups and downs

Learning objective
Read and interpret poems in which meanings are implied or multi-layered.

Word Cloud

chanting	transfer
half time	villain
playground	
scored	

John Foster started to make up poems for his children to stop them from getting bored on long car journeys.

The Price of Fame

It's not easy being famous.

Last week I was a hero.
In injury time
my namesake scored the winner
5 with a glancing header.

Everyone ran round the playground
chanting my name.

Today I'm a villain.
10 Last night I missed an open goal.
Then, just after half time,
I was sent off for a professional foul.
We lost two-nil.

Everyone's blaming me and calling me names.

If it goes on like this,
I'm going to ask Sir for a transfer.

John Foster

Comprehension

A

Give evidence from the text to support your answers.

1 Which line tells us how the player was treated as a hero? Which as a villain?

2 Which line within the poem tells us what this poem is really about?

3 The title of the poem is 'The Price of Fame'. What alternative title would also give the reader an idea of what the poem is about?

Glossary

foul when you have played unfairly during football

injury time extra time at the end of a football match

namesake somebody with the same name as you

nil means no score

Sir formal way of greeting a teacher or sports coach

Practise your poetry

Learning objective
Vary vocabulary, expression and tone of voice to engage the listener and suit the audience, purpose and context.

Kenn Nesbitt is an American writer of humorous children's poetry.

When Sarah Surfs the Internet

When Sarah surfs the Internet
She starts by checking mail.
She answers all her messages
from friends in great detail.

5 She plays a game or maybe two,
and watches a cartoon,
then chats with kids in places
Like Rwanda and Rangoon.

She reads about her favourite bands.
10 She buys an MP3.
She downloads movie trailers
And she looks for stuff for free.

She reads about celebrities
and dreams of wealth and fame,
15 then watches music videos
and plays another game.

If you should say, "Your time is up.
I need to use the net."
She always whines, "I haven't got
20 my homework finished yet."

Kenn Nesbitt

A

1 Write three comprehension questions for your class about the poem.

2 Read the poem aloud together as a class. Decide together how to make a performance reading of the poem, taking turns to read lines in loud or soft voices. Use gestures to act it out.

Writing an interview

Learning objective
Use the styles and conventions of journalism to write reports.

First News interviews Justin Bieber on
Monday 11 April 2011

First News is a children's newspaper which is published on paper and online. In an interview with singer Justin Bieber, the questions a journalist asked made him happy to talk.

Journalists prepare their questions carefully to help them get the answers they want. If the interviewee feels relaxed, they'll say more.

Journalistic writing is different from other types of writing in these ways:

- the level of formality;
- It includes the use of personal language, slang and idiom, because the interview is spoken.
- It has a question and answer pattern, with many of the answers longer than the questions.
- The writing is precise even when the spoken interview may not have been. You don't read lots and lots of 'erms...well... um...' or repetition in written interviews.

Examples
Look at these two sets of questions and answers from the interview.

Question: Do you still get grounded by your mum?
Answer: Yeah, I do.

Question: What is it you think that fans will take from your new film?
Answer: Hopefully they'll see that anything is possible—whether you want to be a doctor or a lawyer or a dancer or whatever you want to do. As long as you stay focused, never say never, and always focus on your dreams, then anything is possible. That's what I want them to see—that this is a dream and dreams do come true.

Glossary
focused have very clear aims
grounded have to stay at home; not allowed out
interviewee the person being interviewed

a How are the two answers different? Why do you think that is?

b Which question do you think is better? Why?

c How long do you think an interview would take if the questions were all like the first one? Would there be much to write about?

The first question only needs a short answer. It's a **closed question**. The second question encourages the interviewee to say much more. It's an **open question**.

2 Look at these questions and say if you think they will encourage a short or a long answer.

   a Where did you grow up?

   b Tell me about your family.

   c Who taught you to play the guitar?

   d You are going on a world tour this year. Can you tell us more about it?

Short closed questions often begin with who, what, why, when, how. Open questions might begin with:

> Tell me all about/more about…

> Can you explain how…

> What were your reasons for…

3 Look at pictures A and B.

   For each picture, write two questions that will get short answers and two questions that will get longer answers.

   Example: Where were you born? (short answer)

   Example: Explain how you started writing stories/playing football. (long answer)

Your writing

Imagine that you work for a newspaper and you are very excited because you are going to interview somebody you like. Think of a name for your newspaper.

1 Write down the name of the newspaper.

2 Create a headline for the interview, for example, 'Maria Angelo talks to Joseph Miguel'.

3 Write a fact file about your interviewee: age, gender, background, biography, achievements, best of times, worst of times, etc. These should just be bullet points.

4 Draft two short answer questions to start, then four long answer questions. Leave plenty of space for your answers.

5 Ask another student to be your interviewee. They could read through the `fact file' so they know how to answer the questions. Write up their answers.

6 Work with a friend and interview each other, using your plans.

> ### Challenge
>
> Interview one of your grandparents, or the oldest person whom you know, for your history class. Find out as much as possible about his or her life.

10 Learning for life

Let's Talk

The Tree of Knowledge is an old metaphor.

1 Why do you think knowledge is shown as a tree?

2 Which picture do you like best? Why?

3 Which picture puzzles you most? What do you think it means?

"Aim for success, not perfection. Never give up your right to be wrong, because then you will lose the ability to learn new things and move forward with your life."
David M. Burns

Eager to learn

Learning objective
Pay close attention in discussion to what others say, asking and answering questions to introduce new ideas.

Word Cloud

atmosphere   knowledge
clues   education
discipline   strict
examinations

A

1 Look at the two pictures on this page. With a partner, find two clues in each one that shows the children are in, or on their way to, school?

2 With your partner, agree on a caption—a word, phrase or sentence for each of the five photos on these pages.

B

You need to prepare a talk about your school to explain to a group of visitors from other countries how education in your country works.

1 Make a list of what to include, for example: school starting and finishing age, school uniforms, school transport, books, computers and examinations.

2 Explain to a partner why you have chosen those items in question 1.

3 Present your ideas to another pair of students and answer their questions about your plan.

C

What do you think?

What makes a good school? With your partner decide what is most important to you.

- tests and exam preparation
- discipline
- good manners
- cooperation with the wider community
- caring atmosphere
- sports facilities
- kind teachers
- strict teachers
- fun clubs and extra activities
- music department
- good examination results

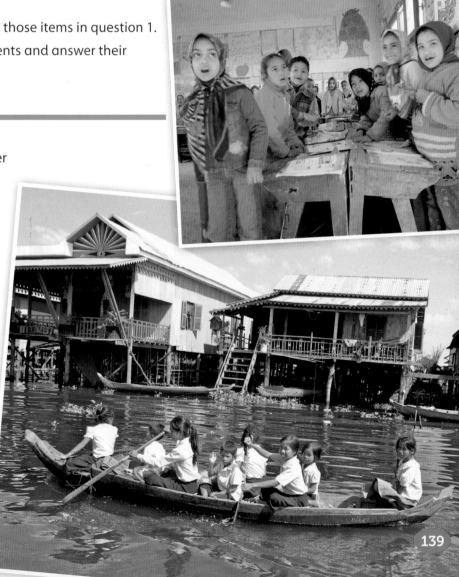

139

Science fiction

Learning objective
Understand aspects of narrative structure such as the handling of time.

It is the year 2155. Tommy, a boy of thirteen, has found an old book. He shows it to his friend Margie.

The Mechanical Teacher

She said, "Where did you find it?"

"In my house." He pointed without looking, because he was busy reading. "In the attic."

"What's it about?"

5   "School."

Margie was scornful. "School? What's there to write about school? I hate school."

Margie always hated school, but now she hated it more than ever. The mechanical teacher had been giving her test after test in
10 geography, and she had been doing worse and worse until her mother had shaken her head sorrowfully and sent for the County Inspector. He was a round little man with a red face and a whole box of tools with dials and wires. He smiled at Margie and gave her an apple, then took the teacher apart. Margie had hoped he wouldn't know how to
15 put it together again, but he knew how all right, and, after an hour or so, there it was again, large and black and ugly, with a big screen on which all the lessons were shown and the questions were asked. That wasn't so bad. The part Margie hated most was the slot where she had to put homework and test papers. She always had to write them out
20 in a punch code they made her learn when she was six years old, and the mechanical teacher calculated the mark in no time.

The Inspector had smiled after he was finished and patted Margie's head. He said to her mother, "It's not the little girl's fault, Mrs. Jones. I think the geography sector was geared a little too
25 quick. Those things happen sometimes. I've slowed it up to an average ten-year level. Actually, the overall pattern of her progress is quite satisfactory." And he patted Margie's head again.

Margie was disappointed. She had been hoping they would take the teacher away altogether. They had once taken Tommy's
30 teacher away for nearly a month because the history sector had blanked out completely.

So she said to Tommy, "Why would anyone write about school?"

Tommy looked at her with very superior eyes. "Because it's not our kind of school, stupid. This is the old kind of school that they had hundreds and hundreds of years ago." He added loftily, pronouncing the word carefully, "*Centuries* ago."

From *Earth is Room Enough*, by Isaac Asimov

Comprehension

A

Explain your answers using words and phrases from the text.

1 Which phrase clearly shows Margie's feelings about school?
2 How do we know that Margie had to do more than one geography test?
3 Why did Margie's mum request that the County Inspector came?
4 Which phrase on line 21 tells the reader that the mechanical teacher worked out pupils' answers quickly?

B

What do you think?

1 Tommy is reading a book about school in the past. What clue is the reader given that books are hard to get hold of?
2 The extract starts in one period of time, then goes back to the past, then back to the original period of time. Find and copy a sentence which shows that the time has switched to the past.
3 Why might Margie not like the Inspector patting her head?
4 There are no human teachers, so how do mechanical teachers get their knowledge?
5 Tom and Margie seem quite different from each other. List three of these differences in a table like the one below.

Tommy	Margie

C

What about you?

1 What do you think is good or bad about a mechanical or digital teacher?
2 If you could program a mechanical teacher, what subjects would you put into it?

141

Apostrophes

> **Learning objective**
> Use apostrophes accurately for omission and possession.

Apostrophes are used in two ways.

▶ To show that letters have been missed out of a word (apostrophes for omission)

Example: it's = it is

▶ To show that something belongs to something or someone else (apostrophes for possession)

Example: The pen belonging to the man = the man's pen

A

1 From the extract on pages 140–1, find five examples of the apostrophe used to show letters have been missed out. (apostrophe for omission)

2 From the extract, find two examples of the apostrophe being used to show that something belongs to something else. (apostrophe for possession)

Top Tip

If there is more than one owner and an -s is added, the apostrophe comes after the -s... **Example**: the shoes belonging to several boys = the boys' shoes.

B

Decide if apostrophes in these sentences are used correctly, and if not write them correctly.

1 Rodriguez's mother's Australian.

2 It's not the little girl's fault.

3 The mechanical teacher has lost it's data.

4 The trees leaves have fallen to the ground.

5 Tommys teachers pen was on the table.

6 The boys' father is looking for him.

7 Next weeks' school council meeting has been cancelled.

8 Thats not mine. That's Tommy's.

9 Margie said that everything has to go in its place.

C

Insert the missing apostrophes in the sentences below.

The boys rucksacks were found by the dogs bed. Marias mother also discovered all the ladies handbags by the dogs bed. Why? Whats going on? Whos to blame? Its a mystery. Theres no doubt about it.

Direct speech

A

Use the sentences of dialogue below as a model. Explain the rules for how speech and dialogue should be punctuated and set out. There should be four rules.

She said, "Where did you find it?"

"In my house." He pointed without looking, because he was busy reading. "In the attic."

"What's it about?"   *A new line is used to show a new speaker*

"School."

Margie was scornful. "School? What's there to write about school? I hate school."

B

Below is another extract from *Earth is Room Enough*, by Isaac Asimov. Write out the lines and add in missing punctuation and some reporting clauses, such as 'he said' and 'she shouted'.

She read the book over his shoulder for a while, then said, "Anyway, they had a teacher

"Sure they had a teacher, but it wasn't a *regular* teacher. It was a man

A man? How could a man be a teacher"

"Well, he just told the boys and girls things and gave them homework and asked them questions

"A man isn't smart enough"

"Sure he is My father knows as much as my teacher."

"He cant A man can't know as much as a teacher.

C

In comics, the words in the speech bubble are the words actually spoken. Make up two speech frames for a comic strip about *The Mechanical Teacher*.

Remembering first days at school

Learning objective
Explore autobiography and first person narration.

Achieng in Kenya

Jambo!
I am a girl from the Luo tribe in Kenya. My name, Achieng, means 'sun', because
5 I was born at midday. On my first day at school, everyone was busy with chores. The girls swept the floor while the boys cut the grass with pangas or long knives. We sat on a straw mat for lessons. For lunch, we
10 ate mandazi (fried bread) and then played football. We used termite nests for the goalposts. This year, I'm going to learn to read and write Kiswahili, also arithmetic and health.

Facts Kenyan children go to school six days a week from January till November. Books and paper are scarce in the rural areas.

Anton in Kazakhstan

Salam Aleikum!
I am Anton and I send you greetings from Almaty, Kazakhstan. September 1st
5 was my first day of school. How excited I was. My father presented me with a bag of candles, pencils and sweets in honour of this important day. On our way to school, which was called 'Number 115',
10 my mother gave me a coin to buy a bouquet of flowers from the bazaar for the teacher. I started to learn to read and write Kazakh and Russian.

Facts On the first day of school, each child brings flowers for the teacher. A new child is chosen to be carried around the room and introduced to the others.

Misaki in Japan

Konichiwa!
I am Misaki from Japan and I remember my first day of school. I was both afraid and excited. I wondered if my classmates would like me and
5 *if the homework would be too hard. As first graders, we learnt Japanese, arithmetic, sewing, music and art. Before going into my classroom, I took off my shoes and put on a pair of slippers. Everyone bowed to the teacher. She showed us how to make an origami*
10 *bird by folding paper.*

Facts Children study Japanese characters, or word pictures, called kanji. They learn more than 1,000 kanji while they are in primary school.

from *It's Back to School We Go!* by Ellen Jackson

Glossary

Jambo greeting in Kiswahili, a language of Kenya

Konichiwa greeting in Japanese

mandazi a type of fried dough commonly eaten in Kenya

origami the Japanese art of folding paper to make attractive shapes

Salam Aleikum greeting in Kazakhstan and other Muslim countries

Comprehension

> **Learning objective**
> Explore autobiography and first person narration.

A

Give evidence from the text to support your answers.

1 What phrases in the letters from Japan and Kazakhstan show that students honoured their teachers?

2 Which phrase from Misaki showed she had mixed feelings about her first day in school?

B

What do you think?

1 Give three possible reasons to explain why books and paper are scarce in some primary schools.

2 Copy the table below. Complete it with examples from the children's letters for each autobiography feature.

Autobiography features	Evidence from letters
Personal pronouns	
Personal details	
Setting the scene, location, time of year	
Event description	
Personal feelings	

C

What about you?

1 Write two experiences from each school which are different from your own first day at school, and one that is the same.

2 Using your table of autobiography features to help you, write a short paragraph about your first day at school. Remember to explain any words which are specific to your country. Add two facts to go with your paragraph.

Word Cloud

arithmetic   scarce
bouquet   slippers
chores   termite
panga

Challenge
Reflect on how you have changed as a learner since your first day at school.

Discussion time
In some countries students take turns to help prepare school meals and clean the school rooms and grounds. Is this a good or bad idea? Explain your opinion with examples.

Verbs

 Learning objective
Revise different word classes.

Verbs are an essential word class. Without a verb, a sentence is not possible. Even one word can be a sentence, if that word is a verb.
Example: Stop!

A

Verbs express actions. Pick out the verbs in these sentences.

1 Each child brings flowers for the teacher.

2 The girls swept the floor while the boys cut the grass with pangas or long knives.

3 I took off my shoes and put on a pair of slippers. Everyone bowed to the teacher.

Verbs also express states, often called 'being' words or 'stative' verbs.
Example: The child **is** ill with fever.

B

Pick out the verbs in these sentences. Then find six more stative verbs in the non-fiction extract.

1 Your classmate seems very nice.

2 We were all there on time.

3 The loss of the school rucksack was my fault.

4 Anton became quite excited about the first day at school.

A finite verb has a subject and can express tense.
Example: She **walked** to school.

A non finite verb, called an infinitive or participle, doesn't show a distinction in tense and needs a phrase or clause.
Example: Before **going** into my classroom, I took off my shoes and put on a pair of slippers.

C

Complete the following sentences, both of which use a non-finite verb.

1 While running to school, she...

2 While travelling to school, she...

Top Tips

▶ **Stative** verbs describe states or conditions which **continue over a period of time.**

Example: I've always liked arithmetic.
and NOT
I've always been liking arithmetic.

▶ **Dynamic** or **action** verbs describe things that happen **within a limited time**, things which have a definite beginning and end. **Come, bring, buy, get, learn, listen** and **watch** are all examples of dynamic verbs.

Example: I **shall be bringing** Anton with me when I visit you on Friday, if that's all right.

Active and passive verbs

> **Learning objective**
> Explore use of active and passive verbs within a sentence.

Verbs can also be in the active and passive voice. If the subject of the verb is doing the action of the verb it is in the **active** voice.

Example: Everyone **bowed to** the teacher.

If the subject of the verb is receiving the action of the verb, the verb is in the **passive** voice.
Example: The teacher **was bowed to** by everyone.

A

Change these sentences to the passive voice.

1 The Headteacher has written an important letter.
2 Heavy rain flattened every plant.
3 The school chef makes delicious cakes.
4 The boys had cleaned all the classrooms.
5 Everyone at the school loves holidays.

B

Rewrite these sentences in the active voice.

1 The bag was found on the bus by Anton.
2 Bags must be left on the hooks by students.
3 Carlos was beaten by Achieng in the tennis match.
4 The front of the school was hidden by trees.
5 School dinners must be eaten slowly by students.

C

Finish the text by writing the passive form of the verb, given in brackets. The first one has been done for you.

Schools (find) *are found* all over the world.

1 Students (take) to school by their parents or carers.
2 The new school (open) by a famous author.
3 A school newsletter (sent) to all students.
4 The school (close) since yesterday.

Dream big!

Learning objective
Articulate personal responses to reading, with close reference to the text.

Word Cloud
ambition   steal
dreams   soul
sights   tear

Paul Cookson wrote this poem for 11-year-olds about to leave primary (elementary) school and go on to secondary (high) school.

Let No-one Steal Your Dreams

Let no-one steal your dreams
Let no-one tear apart
That burning of ambition
4 That fires the drive inside your heart.

Let no-one steal your dreams
Let no-one tell you that you can't
Let no-one hold you back
8 Let no-one tell you that you won't.

Set your sights and keep them fixed
Set your sights on high
Let no-one steal your dreams
12 Your only limit is the sky.

Let no-one steal your dreams
Follow your heart
Follow your soul
For only when you follow them
17 Will you feel truly whole.

Set your sights and keep them fixed
Set your sights on high
Let no-one steal your dreams
21 Your only limit is the sky.

Paul Cookson

Comprehension

A

Use words and phrases from the poem to explain your answers.

1 Rewrite the meaning of the first verse into four sentences of your own words.
2 What does 'set your sights on' mean?
3 Which five things in the poem must you not let people do to you?

B

Poet's use of language

1 Which two words does the poet use in verse 1 to describe heat?
2 Which two phrases does the poet use in verse 3 to indicate 'there's no upper limit'?

C

What about you?

How did the poem make you feel? Give phrases from the poem as part of your explanation.

Language to persuade

Learning objective
Use spoken language well to persuade or make a case.

A

In this activity, you will have informal discussions, first in pairs, then in groups of three. The object is to get others to agree with you.

Look at the table below to see all the arguments against a particular activity. Think of ways to persuade your partner to take up the activity despite their arguments.

Do a cross-country hike	Take part in a school play	Join a sports team
I might get lost / cold / tired / wet...	I'm bound to forget my lines / where to move...	I'm not fast / tall... enough.
I don't like walking.	I wouldn't look right for the part.	I'd let my team-mates down.
	Others could do it better.	Others are better than me.

B

Role play

1 Work in pairs. The 'Player' chooses an activity which she or he feels negative about. The 'Selector' persuades the 'Player' that she or he can do it very well.

2 Change roles. Talk about a different activity.

3 Work on a three-way role-play, with a Selector, a Player and the Supporter, who offers help and gives encouragement.

Example:

Selector: I hope you'll take part in my end-of-term production.

Player: I'm not sure. I've never done any acting.

Support: Why not? You'd be great! Besides, you're good at making us laugh.

Writing a handbook

Learning objective
Select appropriate non-fiction style and form to suit specific purposes.

Guided writing

You have been asked by your Headteacher to write part of a student handbook which is given to new students coming to the school. You need to write key facts about the school, but also some helpful advice, such as how to make friends or what school rules are especially important.

Copy the paragraph boxes below and their subheadings, then make notes inside each. Some ideas have been given to help you.

Paragraph 1 Some key facts about the school

- name of school
- name of Headteacher
- subjects studied
- some information about the actual school building e.g. two floors, gymnasium, science laboratories
- number of pupils
- teachers' names and year groups
- facilities like sport, creative arts
- school uniform
- some key achievements/awards
- you could include a map drawing of inside the school.

Paragraph 2 The school day

- what time the school starts
- morning assembly -or whole school meeting
- how pupils are registered
- break and lunch times - with tips on how to get there on time/ get a place in the queue.
- what snacks or meals you recommend
- lesson finishing time
- times for after school clubs

Paragraph 3 Lessons and Learning

- a learning experience you have had which you will never forget or a favourite teacher or subject you enjoyed
- extracurricular activities available and annual competitions
- advice on homework and preparing for tests
- advice on how to be organized and reflective about your own learning to do their best

Paragraph 4 Final advice and suggestions

- behaviour rules new pupils must follow
- what to do if you feel lost, lonely, sick or have a problem
- how to encourage parents / carers to be involved with your school

Your writing

1 Now write the four-paragraph leaflet properly, using the sub-headings and notes above. Remember to write in the first person, using your own voice (I…). Use personal pronouns (you…) so that new students feel they are being spoken to directly by an older friend.

Edit your writing

2 After you have finished, check your writing. Use the essential and desirable success criteria below. Ask another student to read your leaflet and suggest corrections or improvements.

Essential writing success criteria	Check
Paragraphs should contain what is in the headings only, and not include something else which should be in another paragraph.	
Personal pronouns should be used to give the effect of a voice speaking directly to the new pupils.	
Opinions, where they can be helpful, have been added to the facts.	
Have connectives been used to link ideas for the reader? *Example*: Firstly, I would like to tell you… Adding to that…What's more…	
Have capital letters, full stops and commas been used correctly?	

Desirable success criteria	Check
Vary sentence lengths, with some short sentences for key facts.	
Vary the beginnings to sentences: • Firstly, ____ (using an adverb) • At the back of the school, there is ____ (prepositional phrase) • Although ____ (using a connective) • Running in corridors will get you into trouble. (using a present participle)	

151

Revise and check ❸

Vocabulary

1 Write down the names of three kinds of circus acts.

2 Which part of speech – 'noun', 'verb', or 'past participle' – is each of the following?

celebrate   preparation   decoration   greeting   introduce   presented

3 Write out the sentences below adding the correct idiom from the list.

to cut a long story short   from scratch   speaking my mind   tip of my tongue

a I made the cake _____

b _____ I broke my leg falling on the ice.

c Sometimes I get into trouble for _____ without thinking.

d I can't remember her name but it's on the _____

Punctuation

1 Write out the sentences inserting the missing apostrophes.

a Its not my fault!

b The childrens party was last week.

c Next weeks skating lesson is on Tuesday.

d Thats not mine. Its Sorayas.

2 Punctuate the dialogue below. Start each speech on a new line.

Hello Achieng. Hello Jacob. Did you have a good holiday? Great thanks, we went to Mombasa to see my auntie. Did you stay there for the whole holiday? No, I had to help my mother in our shop in Nairobi for four weeks.

3 Write out these sentences using the correct punctuation from the list.

commas   brackets   colon

a The Vietnamese festival Trung Thu is celebrated in autumn.

b Here is an example path sounds like bath

c The petite very small skater whirled around the rink.

Grammar

1 **Add the correct connectives to the sentences..**

while   as soon as   before   after

a _____ going to bed, she had a glass of water.

b _____ dinner Kim played computer games.

c _____ driving to school, we saw my friend Bo.

d _____ we get home, I'll feed the dog.

2 **Write out the passive form of these sentences.**

a The students (take) to the party by their parents.

b The new gym (opened) by a famous footballer.

3 **Write two sentences for each of these present participles. In one sentence put it in the middle, in the other put it at the beginning.**

a running

b crying

c shouting

Spelling

1 **Write a sentence for each pair of homophones.**

a their   there

b meat   meet

c knows   nose

d flower   flour

2 **Write the meaning of each prefix below, then write one word which uses it.**

micro- auto- trans- sub- im- dis- super- tele-

3 **Write down four words which end in a "k" sound.**

Pulling together

Oki was the finest young hunter of his people. He could run like the wind and carry great loads on his back. He could pull fish from the coldest sea, and there was no one who could paddle a kayak
5 with such speed and skill.

Oki's older sister was called Anuat. She was restless and adventurous. She liked running out along the shore, hunting small birds and taking them home to eat.

"I want to see life!" she used to say to Oki. "It's so dull
10 here at home. I want to meet other people and go to far off places."

Oki's little sister was called Puja. She liked being at home and helping her mother. They would cut up the meat which Oki brought home, cook it and sew clothes
15 from the animal skins.

One winter's day, when the sea was quite frozen over, Oki and the older sister, Anuat, went off over the ice towards some distant islands.

"A fox! Look there! I'll catch him if I can!" shouted
20 Oki, and he raced away, as fast as a wind-blown bird.

The fox was fast, and the chase went on for many miles, but at last Oki captured his prey. Pleased with himself, he trudged back to the place where he had left his sister.

She wasn't there. He looked out over the frozen white
25 world and called as loudly as he could.

No one answered.

Then Oki saw marks in the snow. There were long double stripes made by a sledge's runners, and between

them were the prints of reindeer hooves. All around, the snow had been churned up, as if there had been a struggle.

"What can this mean?" he puzzled. "Has my sister been kidnapped? Why are there prints of reindeer hooves between the marks of the sledge runners?"

Baffled, Oki went home, hoping to find his sister already there. But she hadn't returned. For days and days the family waited and hoped, but Anuat never came back.

Weeks passed, then months. No one talked about Anuat any more, but she was in Oki's mind all the time.

"I must find her. I must!" he said to himself.

Spring was coming now and the warm weather was melting the ice between the islands. Oki gazed out across the vast stretches of icy water. "If Anuat is still alive, she must be far away," he thought sadly.

But Oki was determined to find his sister. He thought
45 long and hard.

"When the sea freezes again, I will set out. But how can I avoid hunger and exhaustion? If only I could move more quickly over the ice."

Oki thought back to the reindeer prints between the
50 sledge marks. The seed of an idea planted itself in his mind. Was it possible? There was only one way to find out …

The next time that Oki went hunting, he took with him a sledge and some strong cords.

"Where are you going?" little Puja asked him. "What are
55 those cords for?"

"You'll see," said Oki, and off he ran, pulling the sledge after him.

It was days before he came home. From inside their snow house, Puja heard a strange noise. She ran outside to look
60 and screamed with fright.

"Father, Mother! Oki's come home, and he's brought a monster with him!"

Her parents ran to look.

"This isn't a monster," laughed Oki.
65 "It's a baby bear, and I'm going to train him to pull my sledge."

Oki's father shook his head and smiled at his son's folly. Oki didn't care. He made a harness for the little white bear and taught him to run
70 ahead of the sledge pulling it along behind him. But the bear cub tired quickly and soon lost interest. So off Oki went again.

A few days later, he came back. This time, unearthly howls brought Puja running out to look. She screamed even louder than before.

"Look at its teeth, and its great round eyes, and its horrid bushy tail!"

"It's nothing to be scared of!" scolded Oki. "What a baby you are! It's only a wolf cub. Now let's see what he can do."

Oki harnessed the bear cub and the wolf cub together, and tried to make them pull the sledge. But they fought each other, biting and scratching. They refused to make the sledge run at all.

Oki didn't give up. He made a special harness so that the two young animals couldn't reach each other. He petted them, and gave them good food, and at last he made them run together. But the wolf ran fast, and the bear ran slowly. The sledge went round in circles!

Oki tried again. He caught another wolf cub, and this time he trained all three to run together, with the bear in the middle. Now it was going well! Oki could ride on his sledge far and fast, and carry heavy loads, too.

* * *

Winter came again. The sea was once more frozen
95 into a vast sheet of ice. The sun hung low in the sky, and
night fell almost before it was day. Oki made a new sledge,
stronger and faster than his old one.

"I'm going to look for my sister," he told his parents. "I
won't rest till I've found her."

100 His father and mother were worried.

"We've lost one of our children," they said. "How could
we bear to lose another? Stay at home, son. Forget your
sister. She is lost to us forever."

But Oki was determined. "I have my animals now
105 to help me," he said. "We can cover miles and miles in
one day."

He set off, racing fast to the place where he had last seen
his sister, out on the ice that covered the sea.

Soon, the bear was tired and slowed the others down, so
110 Oki unhitched him and carried him on the sledge.

Now, with the wolves alone, the sledge shot forwards, swishing across the ice faster than any person could run. On and on went the wolves, while Oki cracked his whip over their willing backs and shouted cries of encouragement.

And so they crossed the sea, until at last they came to the far shore where the ground was rough and uneven. It was impossible to run the sledge over it.

Oki hitched his sledge to an iceberg and gave each of his animals a big chunk of meat to eat. Then on he went on foot, alone. He was tired and hungry but he wouldn't turn back.

"I'll find you, Anuat. I'll find you!" he muttered to himself through the freezing wind that ruffled the fur edging to his hood.

At last, he came to a settlement of igloos. A woman came out at his call. It was Anuat herself, and in her arms was a baby, all muffled up in fur.

"Oki!" she cried, her face lighting up with delight. "How did you get here? How did you find me?"

159

He followed her into her igloo, and the brother and sister talked long into the night.

"That day," Anuat said, "when you ran off after the fox, some strangers came past. They snatched me up
135 and carried me away on their sledge. It was pulled by a reindeer, so we were soon far beyond anywhere I had been before. I fought and struggled, but they wouldn't let me go.

"Eventually we reached this land and I was forced to
140 stay. But then I met a good kind man here. We fell in love and married. Look, we have a baby now! There was only one thing that was making me unhappy, and that was the thought of my family, worried and wondering where I was.

"Now you have come all this way to find me! But how
145 did you do it, Oki? How did you come so far across the sea ice, on your own?"

"I'll show you in the morning, if you'll come down to the edge of the sea ice with me," said Oki, yawning. "But now, dear sister, I want something to eat. In fact, I
150 want a feast! So let me see what's in that pot bubbling so hard on the fire. I could eat a whole seal all by myself!"

And from that day to this, people have used the descendants of wolves to pull their sledges across the frozen Arctic landscapes.

Elizabeth Laird